HYMN LINES

75 Devotional Thoughts
Based on Lines and Phrases
from Great Hymns and Songs
of the Christian Faith

R. G. HUFF

ISBN: 9781698321530
Published by WorshipRx.com
Waxahachie, TX

Cover Design: Billy Coburn

Photos of R. G. Huff: Lowry Studios

I love the great hymns of the Christian faith. I love singing them, and I love reading the words. When a grand tune is well-married to a great text, congregational singing is a wonderful experience!

It occurred to me a few years ago that in most hymns, there is one line or one phrase which seems to rise from others and seems to speak to me more intensely or at a deeper level than the other words. In the truly well-crafted hymns, there may be several of these special, sacred moments in the lyrics. These were the worship times within the songs that I began to relish more than the rest... and I started calling these phrases or word-groups "hymn lines."

When people asked me, "What's your favorite hymn?" I realized I didn't necessarily have a favorite full hymn, but I had a whole bunch of favorite hymn lines. Based on those lines, I developed some devotional thoughts... or musings... and those became a blog... and now I'm putting some of them into printed form so folks can keep them by their bedside or on the table by their easy chair or on their office desk -- wherever they might stop to think about their faith during the day, especially if they, like me, love the great hymns we've sung since childhood and revere to this day.

If you are one of those people, I hope you'll enjoy the 75 entries I've included from the over 400 I've written. Paring them down was the hardest part. Some of the hymns I've selected have more than one pithy hymn line, but I've forced myself to choose just one from each for this project.

You may want to keep a hymnal handy so you can read the hymn line in context... and so you can rear back and sing if you want to!

Every now and then you'll come across a hymn you may not know... one they don't sing in your faith tradition. Don't skip over it. You might learn something that will strengthen your own journey.

I have tried to be careful to be gender neutral in all my discussions of humankind. However, for my purposes here, I have kept all references to God as a male, using he, him, his pronouns and referring to God as Father. This is very much in keeping with most of the language of the hymns with which I deal, and it simplified my process of having to remember to be theo-politically sensitive at every turn.

R. G. Huff

Why should I be discouraged?
I sing because I'm happy.
His eye is on the sparrow,
and I know he watches me.

Civilla D. Martin (1866~1948)

1 Holy, Holy, Holy

Tune: NICAEA
Text: Reginald Heber (1783-1826)

"Only thou art holy. There is none beside thee perfect..."

Our God truly is "one of a kind." No one else is perfectly holy. I think that goes without saying… but it cannot go without singing!

Every congregation of all denominations knows – and probably loves – this great hymn that reminds us of the "otherness" of God. It points us to that *mysterium tremendum*: that overwhelming mystery of who God is. ▷ *overwhelming Awe by such a mystery*

Besides God, there is none perfect. Only God is holy.

As early church theologian St. Nicolas Cabasilas put it, our God is
- more affectionate than any friend,
- more just than any ruler,
- more loving than any parent,
- more a part of us than our own limbs,
- more necessary to us than our own heart.

This one-of-a-kind holy otherness is what attracts many of us to God. We stand awestruck in God's presence, finding it unfathomable that there should be One like this. Sturdy hymns like "Holy, Holy, Holy" usher us into that presence; few jazzed-up arrangements maintain that sense of awe – same words, same basic melody, but not the same astonishment!

Beyond that, however, we are equally amazed that such a holy Other could be interested in us… that God would condescend to humankind to draw us to himself. It is awe upon awe – wonder of wonders – truly amazing!

Such awareness puts us in our place and raises him to his rightful place: high and holy. Besides him, there is none other qualified. *Perfect in power, in love and purity.*

2   **Savior, Like a Shepherd Lead Us**

Tune: BRADBURY
Text: Dorothy A. Thrupp (1779-1847)

"Early let us seek thy favor. Early let us do thy will."

Are you a morning person? I am. I tend to get a lot accomplished in the earliest part of the day. Generally speaking, I don't sleep very well; so I am not the kind who leaps out of bed to cheerfully greet the morning! But once I'm up and have a couple of cups of freshly-ground coffee in my system, I'm probably at my best. I used to wish that choir rehearsals were first thing on Wednesday mornings instead of the last thing on Wednesday evenings!

This hymn line from a lady who was born in England at the end of the American Revolution opens the final stanza of a hymn which is loved by most all Christian congregations. It encourages us to go ahead and get on with our seeking of Christ's favor and the doing of his will. Pleasing the blessed Lord is something we should not wait around to do.

We can look at this as a call to seek out God early on in our pilgrimage – not to wait too long to step into the kingdom and enjoy the favor of Christ. Or we might see it as a way to begin each day. First thing off the pillow, I may need to say, "I'm going to seek your favor today. I'm going to try to do your will." We might even need to do this at the first of every hour... even the first of every minute... because we sometimes forget!

Either way, let this hymn line remind us to make our continuing relationship with Jesus a first priority in our lives – day by day, hour by hour, minute by minute.

Most of you probably read these early in the day; you use them as a morning devotional thought. If that's the case, it's not too late to start off your day seeking the favor or the One who loved us and who loves us still.

3 No, Not Despairingly

Tune: KEDRON
Text: Horatius Bonar (1808-1889)

"Lord, I confess to thee sadly my sin.
All I am tell I thee, all I have been."

This is one of the most powerful devotional hymns out there anywhere. The text is so thoughtfully deep that most congregational worship leaders avoid it… partly because it can hardly be taken in. Churches that lean more toward the contemplative will find it more useful in public worship. However, it is a text we should read regularly to keep us in check with our relationship with Christ.

To borrow a word from this hymn line, "sadly" not many evangelical churches sing this hymn anymore. That is sad for me because there may be no other complete hymn in all of church history with more profound one-liners than this one. Those "ruminating" texts are why I am committed to hymns – congregational and devotional.

Two of the most introspective sentences in all hymndom are spoken here. Nothing frivolous or superficial. "Sadly, righteous Christ, I admit there are some darknesses in my life that I cannot express out loud to any human. You know about all this already, of course, but I need to tell you the whole truth of who I am and what I've done… who I've been. Here goes…" A chill should have come across you as you pondered that. If not, go back and read it again!

In the hymn, Bonar goes on to ask for purging, washing and cleansing; it is a true confession.

For me, the great mercy of this text is that I can lay it all out there – expose myself, so to speak – and my relationship with Christ will not be affected. Do you realize that? Do you really? This ability of the Savior to continue loving me in spite of the sad shape my life may have been in – I am blown away by that. Absolutely blown away.

Like any good friend, in all likelihood the response of Christ is, "I know. I know. It's okay. We're still okay."

Though too often omitted from public worship, confession is still good for the soul… for THIS poor soul at least.

4 Love Divine, All Loves Excelling

Tune: BEECHER
Text: Charles Wesley (1707-1788)

"Fix in us thy humble dwelling."

I was an art major when I first entered Carson Newman College in the fall of 1967. I had a decent ability to draw things. While being artistic, after completing a section of a charcoal drawing or working in pastels, I took a can of spray fixative, shook it to hear that little ball rattle against the can, and generously covered the possible-masterpiece so it would not smear if accidentally touched while I continued to work on it. The process is called "fixing" the artwork.

We are only three phrases into the singing of "Love Divine, All Loves Excelling" when this hymn line crosses our lips, and because it is so early-on in the hymn, it may not register in our brain what it is we are singing. When I speak these words on the nine assigned pitches, I have a flashback to my art-major days... of being sure I am either outside or in a well-ventilated room in order not to inhale the fumes from the Krylon aerosol can. This was BEFORE people actually wanted to inhale fumes like these!

In the hymning of these words, I am asking God to cover me in such a way that my faith might not smear – or that the distinct lines of my belief system might not become indefinite or undefined. That he might take up residence in my life in such a way that these cannot be disturbed.

Other hymns use the word "seal" to mean the same thing (e.g. "Here's my heart, O take and seal it..."), but I'm glad Wesley chose "fix" – a word with which this artsy person can identify!

Ever since we came to him in faith, God – the ultimate artist – has been drawing his nature across the sketch pad of our lives. Everything he has inscribed there has given us the possibility to be more like him... more like his Son... more Christ-like. I, for one, do not want any of that to be messed up or smeared by anything or anyone who would like to make my Christian experience anything less than beautiful.

God is making a masterpiece within us. That's not self-aggrandizing – that's the truth! And we want to be sure that beauty is preserved… or fixed… unlikely to be damaged. That preservation is more likely to occur if Christ is allowed to take up full-time, humble residence at the center of our lives.

"Fix" can mean to repair something that is broken or not working properly; but in this case, it means to keep it from needing to be repaired!

---

5 Sunshine in My Soul

Tune: SUNSHINE
Text: Eliza E. Hewitt (1851-1920)

"When Jesus shows his smiling face, there is sunshine in my soul."

Many of us suffer from depression at differing levels. Fortunately, for most of us this downheartedness is shallow and short-lived; for others – even strong Christians – melancholy may be a daily state of being. Some live in darker shades of gray. This is not something to take lightly. Our response should never be flippant or unconcerned; "just get over it" should not be our attitude. Honest, non-condescending encouragement is probably our best approach.

For those of us who are not at those deepest depths of despair, turning our eyes upon Jesus may be just the thing to return brightness to our gloom – to trade sunshine for our darkness. So often in our grasping for a glimmer of hope, the smiling face of Christ passes before our spiritual eyes, our attitudes improve, and we are lifted from nighttime to noonday bright.

I'm reminded of the hopeful Psalm passage: "We may weep throughout the night, but with the morning comes joy." (30:5b)

The day may be dreary and the long night may be weary, but be reassured that our Savior cares. May his smiling face come to all of us to redeem us from the pit… to pull us out and bring sunshine to our souls. Then may there be music in our souls today, a carol to our King!

6 When in Our Music God Is Glorified

Tune: ENGLEBERG
Text: Fred Pratt Green (1903-2000)

"Adoration leaves no room for pride." [1]

This new hymn (1972) is one you may have not sung, especially if you are in a projector-driven service where for the most part only the hymns with familiar tunes are included. Even so, this one would be worth teaching to any congregation and making it as familiar as "How Great Thou Art"!

It's common lack of use notwithstanding, Fred Pratt Green's hymn is filled with wonderful phrases about worship – especially the musical elements, and this hymn line drives home a very, very important truth about what happens when engaged in acts of adoration – or worship: *there is no room for the ego!* My personal pride must be set aside in order that I can express how proud I am of God… how much he is revered… what a high value we place on him. In order for him to be magnified (increase), I take the place of humility (decrease). See John 3:30.

To put that into the language of music, I must decrescendo so he can crescendo!

There is no place for show business in the worship business. Entertainment is not commensurate with a spirit of sincere worship. I am startled by it every time I sing this hymn. Fortunately, the congregations I have led most recently have known and appreciated it. I catch myself singing this one on my own – a lot actually – because I need to be reminded of this truth as much as anyone: **hubris and holiness are not compatible.**

To me, this says that when we approach the throne together, we ALL have to 'check our pride at the door.' The narthex of every church in the world should be stacked to the ceiling with pride-backpacks left there by those who have entered the sanctuaries/worship centers. Perhaps we need to install a pride-check closet instead of a coat-check closet!

You've heard the phrase "my pride and joy"? In worship, these two cannot genuinely coexist. We should be going after a pride-less joy. It could revolutionize corporate worship, especially if all of us in the room – the leaders and the participants – all of us would set aside the deadly sin* of pride. When that happens, I think the adoration that emerges might be unprecedented, overwhelming.

It is a more exciting thought than I can get my mind around. I'm sincerely waiting for that to happen one Sunday morning – maybe even this week.

The seven deadly sins are: wrath, greed, sloth, pride, lust, envy, and gluttony. Most would say that pride is at the root of the other six!

---

7   My Faith Looks Up to Thee

Tune: OLIVET
Text: Ray Palmer (1808-1887)

"O may my love to thee pure warm and changeless be."

Rich in language and deep in theology, Ray Palmer has expressed his faith in ways with which I identify and resonate. This is definitely one of those texts that works as a devotional hymn as well as it does as a congregational expression.

The line of this prayer-hymn that I've selected for today helps us understand what it means to love in general… and in this case how our love for Christ is exhibited.

All of us express love in different ways. [If you've never read Gary Chapman's THE FIVE LOVE LANGUAGES, get a copy. It's NOT just a marriage-help book!] Whatever our way of expressing love, these three are foundational:

- **Pure**: not motivated by self-gain, without mixed motive, unpolluted.
- **Warm**: engaging, affectionate, expressive.
- **Changeless**: consistent, never in doubt, unswerving, dependable, stable. →

These define a loving relationship of any kind; these set the standard. They describe God's love for us and kindle within us the longing to reciprocate.

This hymn line is the prayer of my heart. I hope you share that desire.

---

8 Day by Day and with Each Passing Moment

Tune: BLOTT EN DAG
Text: Caroline V. Sandell-Berg (1832-1903)

"Trusting in my Father's wise bestowment, I've no cause for worry or for fear."

This is one of my break-out hymns. It ministered to me at a time in my life when I thought I had hit rock-bottom. No encouraging words or pats on the back could shake me loose. But driving through the streets of Denver playing a cassette (yes, cassette) of Cynthia Clawson singing this hymn brought me to such tears that I had to pull over from the traffic and let it rinse me clean.

This hymn line reminds me that we quite simply have to trust what God has given us, believing that his gifts were bestowed upon us in HIS wisdom for OUR purpose in HIS kingdom. Then we need to gird up our loins and get on with our lives without worry or fear.

I was one of those ministers of music to whom God had not bestowed a glorious singing voice. In fact, although I felt a tugging (a calling) toward the ministry of music, I kept telling myself that I couldn't do that because all my music minister heroes were also great singers. Convinced that I should take it on anyway, I realized that I had some strong gifts for teaching and administration, and those were the backbone of my forty-plus years in that position. I couldn't fall back on my own, personal talent; I had to instead be sure I had everyone else ready. I found that I could coordinate most any event to almost seamless proportions! I trusted my Father's wise bestowment and went for it...rarely, if ever, singing a solo!

Later in the hymn, we sing, "E'er (always) to take as from a father's hand, one by one, the days, the moments fleeting." We recognize that as we see our heavenly Father, Jehovah, handing out the blessings one by one at just the appropriate time to empower us in our weakness. Life is going by at break-neck speed for most of us, and we often feel that nothing is going to rescue us as we perish underneath the load of everyday commitments -- at school, at work, with our family and friends... even at church!

Like the old 1950's TV show, the Father knows best. We have to keep reminding ourselves of that. And because he knows best, we have to trust his wisdom with as little worry and fear as possible. Today, in uncertain moments, repeat this phrase: "Father knows best. Father knows best. Father knows..."

---

9   I Must Tell Jesus

Tune: ORWIGSBURG
Text and Music: Elisha A. Hoffman (1839-1929)

"I cannot bear my burdens alone."

We're taking on a good old gospel song today. Those of us who cut our musical/spiritual teeth on songs like this find ourselves singing them as prayers (aloud or silently), especially just when we need him most. That need may be to share some great, good news – and we run through the hallway joyfully saying, "Who can I tell? Who can I tell?" At other times the need may be just the opposite: we are so weighed down that we don't know with whom we can share such a burden, and we whisper into our chest, "Who can I possibly tell?" That's the kind of situation out of which this text emerges, emphasizing the trials, burdens, distress, troubles, temptation, and evil allurement. And each downcast stanza is followed by the closing words of the refrain: *Jesus can help me, Jesus alone.*

We've all been there, done that… and have found this hymn line to be one of the great truths of our hymnody.

Any time we congregate, we need to be reminded that those people we are about to meet down at the church house are also people who are (hopefully) willing to help us bear our burdens. They are there to **be Christ** for us… and we for them.   →

We meet together as a church family for many reasons – primarily worship of the Everliving One. But let's not overlook this burden-bearing ministry. After all, anything considered a ministry in the church should be a gap where we step in and do what Christ would do if he were still among us in the flesh. Since he is not, he has called us and empowered us by his Spirit to fill in for him. "Bear one another's burdens and fulfill Christ's intention" (Galatians 6:2).

When you start to do any renovation on a building, you have to be careful not to remove a load-bearing wall. Those around you in your church family serve as this load-bearing wall, giving you necessary support. Be careful not to remove them from your life by keeping those burdens to yourself without sharing the load. After all, it comes down to this: none of us can bear our burdens alone. Tell Jesus. He has people on stand-by!

---

10   Jesus, Thy Boundless Love to Me

Tune: ST. CATHERINE
Text: Paul Gerhardt (1607-1676)

"All coldness from my heart remove."

What a prayer! It seems like it needs no further explanation or discussion. But then, this hymn line would be much too short an entry! On the other hand, I know that if this could happen in my life, I would indeed be a different follower of Christ.

I take my praying seriously, and that means I talk to God as openly as possible. In public prayers, I rein myself in as needed depending on my human audience; however, I'm carrying on a conversation with the Almighty while my fellow mere mortals listen in!

I try to not be formulaic in my prayers, but if I did, I should add "All coldness from my heart remove" to all my prayers – public and private.

The great formulaic prayer – the one we call "The Lord's Prayer" or the "Our Father" – includes the phrase *"Forgive us our trespasses as we forgive those who trespass against us."* Our coldness of heart against individuals and/or groups usually stems from having been (in our opinion) wronged. There are those who have left the organized church and are cold toward her because they were at some point disenfranchised over a life choice or a lifestyle – or their honesty. Others of us have placed our heart in the deep freeze over disagreements with family members and former friends.

Speaking of honesty, most of us know the chill-down-the-spine feeling we get when we have to pass certain people in the hallway between Sunday School and worship. The coldness of heart surges into our system, and we try desperately to avert our eyes for fear that our mouth might say what our mind is thinking. Too honest? Am I alone in this? I think not!

Worst of all is the child of God whose very outlook on life has cooled to the point of freezing – the one whose heart is frozen hard as a rock due to countless, endless experiences which have lowered their spiritual temperature to depths they could never have anticipated – and likely would never admit.

We were not redeemed for such an attitude as this. We were 'set on fire' at our salvation-time, and for many of us, the heating scale has been on the decline ever since.

Once upon a time, some angry, disappointed people were traveling on a road from Jerusalem to Emmaus. Along the way, a stranger joined them and allowed them to vent their confusion, their crisis-of-faith. At their destination, they invited the stranger to remain for dinner saying, "Stay with us." At table, they recognized him as the Christ. We know the story; it is one of those we see unfold almost as a staged drama. As the scene concludes, after the main character has left the stage, the actors say to one another, *"Were not our hearts warmed within us as he talked with us…?"* Indeed, when he walks with us and talks with us and tells us we are his own, our hearts begin to thaw.

Lord Jesus, stay with us. Continue the warming of hearts until they are again afire with love and not near-hate for our fellow believers and others outside the faith family. Lord Jesus, stay with us, that we may walk so near yourself that we can do no less than reenact your lifestyle. Lord Jesus, stay with us. All coldness from our hearts remove; may every act, word, thought be love. Amen.

11 All the Way My Savior Leads Me

Tune: ALL THE WAY
Text: Fanny J. Crosby (1820-1915)

"Gushing from the rock before me, lo a spring of joy I see."

The joy of the Lord rarely comes as a trickle.

While writing this second stanza of one of her best-known hymns, Fanny Crosby seems to be channeling the Children of Israel on their Exodus trek. She mentions following the meandering route and being fed the living bread – manna. Then comes this description of their situation:
> *"Though my weary steps may falter,*
> *and my soul athirst may be,*
> *Gushing from the rock before me,*
> *lo a spring of joy I see."*

Although the pilgrimage to the Promised Land is punctuated by an arguable event (whether or not Moses followed Jehovah's directive or whether he took credit for the miracle), this fact remains: water gushed forth from a rock and the people were satiated. Not only were they in a quest to quench their lips, their souls were also athirst.

With the herded Hebrews, we look to the Rock because we wish to be slaked of our soul's dehydration.

This gushing is something to which we can relate in nature – Old Faithful, Niagara Falls, the Holana Blowhole on Oahu – and in man-made fountains, broken water mains, and the Bellagio Hotel. People stand in line to watch these things happen because there is such a display of might and pent-up force. Rarely, if ever, have we stood in line to watch a dripping faucet or a trickling stream.

So it is for us whose inner self is a-dry. The joy of the Lord gushes forth with such potency that we can hardly take it in to its fullness.

Stand back, folks. A gushing spring of joy is on its way!

12 Praise the Savior, Ye Who Know Him

Tune: ACCLAIM
Text: Thomas Ken (1637-1711)

"He for conflict fits and arms us,
Nothing moves and nothing harms us
While we trust in him."

This is not a line from "Onward, Christian Soldiers" or one of the more militant hymn texts. While it may have had some battle implications when Thomas Ken penned these words, their application works for us in our everyday lives which, like it or not, are filled with conflict – some great, some miniscule… but often at the moment seeming insurmountable.

We have put on the whole armor of God from Ephesians 6, haven't we? Aren't we dressed head-to-toe with the belt of truth, vest of righteousness, shoes of readiness, the shield of faith, the helmet of salvation, the sword of the Spirit, and prayer? According to Paul's letter, these will make it possible for us to stand firm in the midst of all kinds of evil.

We have been well-suited to our environment. We are tailor-made to be God's people – fearfully and wonderfully constructed. We need to look to our strengths (above) and not hide behind our weaknesses. Nothing can move us entirely off-balance because we are planted firmly in our relationship with our Designer. We may get roughed up a bit – even injured in the conflict – but no spiritual harm will come to us while we trust in him.

When I got up this morning, I didn't go looking for conflict; but it always seems to find me! You probably feel the same way. Well, let's agree not to let it defeat us. Let's hold up under the struggle, believing that the Tailor has clothed us consummately. His armor is a perfect fit.

When Morning Gilds the Skies

Tune: LAUDES DOMINI
Text: from *Katholiches Gesangbuch*
Translated by Edward Caswall (1814-1878)

"The night becomes as day when from the heart we say, 'My Jesus Christ be praised!'"

There is something about genuine praise of Christ that can most certainly make drastic changes in our demeanor. Praise which takes <u>us</u> out of the picture and places Christ <u>only</u> at the center – praise which is so sincere that we can think of nothing else – praise which for a few moments carries us near to the heart of God: THIS is the kind of praise I'm after.

Whole-hearted praise can truly turn our darkness into light – our night into day – our less-than-happy days into times filled with joy.

In most hymnals, just before this hymn line, at the end of the first stanza, we sing a strange phrase for 21st Century worshipers: "To Jesus I repair." The word repair conjures up thoughts of fixing something that is not working… to have a car repaired, etc. For some of us, that may be exactly what we need to do – to make reparation of damaged territory.

But the better use of the word here might be "to Jesus I resort"… or turn. A less-used definition of the word is simply <u>go</u>: "Let us repair to the parlor after dinner," or (in courtroom talk) "As the lawyers repair to the judge's chambers…"

On the heels of our singing about turning to or going to Jesus, the next line – today's hymn line – speaks of night turning to day when we resort to our Savior with overflowing hearts which desire nothing but expressing our praise for him.

I love that in the very next line of this hymn, the powers of darkness fear when the sweet sound of authentic praise arises! In the same way that God rejoices over us (Zephaniah 3:17) – even dances over us in some translations – the Evil One cowers and sticks his fingers in his ears because he cannot abide the attendant attitude of this kind of praise!

All of a sudden, today's hymn line has been defined by what we just sang and by what we are about to sing. Brief kernels of faith-expressions like these have prompted me to write these entries. We are overlooking some richness of language by quickly passing through even the most-familiar songs in our hymnic vocabulary.

I'm <u>here</u> to remind you to <u>hear</u> what your mouth is <u>saying</u> when you <u>sing</u>... and to let your heart respond accordingly throughout this book.

So, from your heart say (or sing) many, many times, "May Jesus Christ be praised!" See if maybe your darkness turns to light! And then flip that switch as often as you can!

---

14 There's a Wideness in God's Mercy

Tune: WELLESLEY
Text: Frederick W. Faber (1814-1863)

"But we make his love too narrow by false limits of our own."

I think I would have enjoyed getting to know Fredrick Faber. First of all, he was British, so I'm sure he was fascinating... had probably visited Downton Abbey. He was a deep-thinking theologian, and his thoughtfulness is obvious in a couple of his other hymns: "Faith of Our Fathers" and "My God, How Wonderful Thou Art", for instance. I would love to have had tea with him and been able to discuss theology!

This hymn line is so on-target and speaks such a loud message to the church today... a century and a half later. The limiting of God's love is of our own doing; the boundless love of Scripture has been pulled back and boxed in by humankind, and exclusion has replaced inclusion. This troubles me a lot... a whole lot! Where in Holy Writ do we find a teaching of Jesus that tells us to draw a line outside which the love of God is not available? I don't find it.

→

This hymn line is followed by an even more cautionary thought: *"And we magnify his strictness with a zeal he will not own."* Read that again and ponder for a moment those times when we as individuals and congregations and denominations have made way too much of the vengeful, angry, strict... even bullying God -- and forgotten to magnify his loving, forgiving, grace-filled nature. We've done it (according to Faber) with a fervor that God himself will not allow.

I know I've "gone to preaching" here, but this is one of my tallest soapboxes! And this grand old long-dead English poet-theologian verbalizes it so very, very well. If I had the opportunity to sit down to tea with him, I think his spirit would agree with my spirit, and I'd have to say, "You go, Fred!" He'd laugh, I'd blush – then we'd talk more about the nature of God in Christ Jesus.

Father, forgive us for magnifying your strictness when we KNOW you are a merciful, kind, open-armed Deity. Teach us a lesson from this hymn line. Amen.

---

15   Rejoice, Ye Pure in Heart

Tune: MARION
Text: Edward H. Plumptre (1821-1891)

"Yes, on through life's long path, still singing as you go."

Of course, I'm going to be drawn to this hymn line: it's all about singing!

We're not necessarily following the Yellow Brick Road with Munchkins at our ankles, but we are on a lengthening path filled with uncertainties. Oh, I realize we know where we're going to end up, but we can never be quite certain what to expect along the way. To carry that Oz analogy a bit further, some of us are hopelessly positive, skipping down the path in our ruby slippers with great confidence and resolve that we can find our way back home. Others are heartless – or have lost heart. Some are totally without courage. Still others are mindless in their travels, not alert or thoughtful. Then there are the ones who are Toto-ly happy to just follow everyone else, making no decisions of their own.

It is not, however, the Great and Powerful Oz we seek in order to ask for fulfillment. *"Weeee're* (not) *off to see the Wizard!"* Rather we are on the path to *things that are higher, things that are nobler*. We have set our sights on the heavenly vision and pleasing the Ruler of Heaven and Earth is our highest call. Thankfully, he is not hiding behind a curtain pretending to be someone he is not!

I never remember walking alone through a cemetery after dark, but I've seen that in plenty of movies. In all those situations, the one traversing the graves is whistling or humming… or singing as they go. Perhaps they are trying to ward off the imagined evil spirits lurking there – or better yet, the singing will take their mind off the situation in which they find themselves: the music allays their fear.

We share life's long path. Our struggles and difficulties may vary, but if we can face whatever lies ahead with a song – perhaps even a hymn – to take our mind off those things which so easily beset us – we may more likely make it safely to the other side of the graveyard… or the end of the Yellow Brick Road… life's long path.

The word "still" in this hymn line indicates that we have already been singing, and that we should keep it up. "Yes" – with confidence we set out across the uncharted territory, continuously with a song in our heart and on our lips as we *rejoice, give thanks and sing*.

Let's lock arms and head down life's road together-- if not the Yellow Brick Road – heartily vocalizing our common faith in song!

16 Immortal Love, Forever Full

Common Tune: SERENITY
Text: John Greenleaf Whittier (1807-1892)

"We test our lives by thine."

When growing up in Pigeon Forge, there was a place at the top of the stairs leading down into our basement where my mother would occasionally stand me up against the wall, level a ruler on top of my head, and make a mark. Beside that mark, she wrote the date. I was an only child, so I don't know why "Ronald George" was written above all these tick marks. I guess she never measured herself or daddy.

Interestingly as I recall, this was always done at my request – not on my birthday or New Year's Day. Whenever I thought I had grown a little, I would ask to be measured.

The house is still there on Forest Avenue. I wonder if those vertical evaluations are still in that stair well?

In this six-word phrase from a poem by a great American poet icon, we remind ourselves to stop measuring ourselves against other humans and to rather use the example of the Lord and Master of us all.

Seems like every talent/gift I have falls into some artistic category. Throughout my entire educational and professional career I caught myself saying, "I wish I could sing like him," or "I wish I could draw as well as she does," or "If I could act like that other guy, I would have the lead," and so on. I never seemed to measure up. In my personal evaluations, I was a little good at doing a lot of things, but great at nothing.

The truth is that I have way too often applied the same testing process to my spiritual life, wishing I had the prayer-life of another – or the patience, the wisdom, the understanding of scripture, the moral fortitude; I even wondered why I didn't have as much faith as my mentors – those I looked up to.

When I come across this final sentence of Whittier's hymn-text, I want to slap myself for making such comparisons. I should be testing my own life by the benchmarks set up by the One I really look up to: my Savior Example. As with my childhood requests, perhaps I need to ask for a measurement of my spiritual growth.

Judgmental of the spiritual lives of others? Guilty. This hymn line also reminds me that I am not the judge of my fellow strugglers in the faith. I need to get my nose out of their business, stop mouthing off, and set my eyes on Christ. (That's three facial metaphors by the way!) In all those years that Hedy measured the growth of her only son, she never asked any of my friends to come stand there and see how they measured up to my progress; she only measured me against myself.

Focus on how YOU measure up. Stand against the proverbial wall and let your heavenly Parent tick off your progress, regardless of how the kid down the street is progressing!

17   Stir Your Church, O God, Our Father

Tune: MADILL
Text: Milburn Price (1938-   )

"All folk are your creation and… have dignity." [2]

Here is the full hymn line for today:
> Give to us a social conscience
> which enables us to see
> That all folk are your creation
> and that they have dignity.[2]

With ongoing thoughts of human equality in mind, it seems appropriate that we take up this line from Milburn Price's most-sung hymn.

For me, this is a prayer of reminder – one that prompts me to be unjudgmental in my Christian witness. If we are not careful, we will develop prejudicial opinions about people groups (not just racial) who are different from us, and in that bias we can subconsciously marginalize them before we realize it.

→

In staged drama, there is usually a prompter whose job it is to keep up with the script and be at the ready offstage to rescue the actor who disremembers a line and risks throwing off the whole production. The actor KNOWS the lines; he/she just momentarily forgets. Those of us who have stood in that frozen on-stage position are grateful for those who whisper what we know but have momentarily forgotten.

Hymn lines like this assist us in our lapses – those times when we are less than Kingdom people… when we forget our lines… when we are at risk of derailing the cause of Christ. We are jarred back into the social consciousness to which we aspire and are set back onto the better path, adhering to the Script as life's drama unfolds.

18 I Stand Amazed in the Presence of Jesus

Tune: MY SAVIOR'S LOVE
Text and Tune by Charles H. Gabriel (1856-1932)

"My song shall ever be: How marvelous, how wonderful is my Savior's love for me."

First of all, if you are the worship leader at your church, never let the congregation SIT to sing this hymn. Just sayin'!

When the question is asked in a Bible study group, "What is your favorite attribute of God?", the most common response is going to be his love. Some of us will try to come up with something more profound (like omnipresence or immutability), but down deep we simply want to say, "His love for me."

At the end of this entry, I have put Charles Hadden Spurgeon's list of the attributes of God, just in case you're interested!

The first thing the nursery teacher repeated to you in Sunday School was "Jesus loves you." The first song you ever learned was probably "Jesus Loves Me." Hymnal and chorus-books are filled with songs that tell us about how much God loves us… and give us many opportunities to say how much we love him. The love of God is so ingrained in our spirit, our psyche and our vocabulary, we can hardly escape it, even if we tried – and why would we?

As I sing this hymn, each time we come to the refrain, my faith is brightened – even renewed – by the two descriptors: marvelous and wonderful. I've probably sung this hymn a thousand times in my lifetime – corporately or to myself – and still... **still** these two words grab me by the heart and throw me about the room because they are so spot-on and commensurate with my own personal worship love language.

Any time you have fifteen extra seconds today, stop and sing the refrain of this hymn... or sing it while you go about your work. If it doesn't raise the ends of your lips, we need to talk!

C. H. Spurgeon's Attributes of God:
- Eternal
- Faithfulness
- Foreknowing
- Good
- Holy
- Immutable
- Impartial
- Incomprehensible
- Infinite
- Jealous
- Justice
- Longsuffering
- Omnipotent
- Omnipresent
- Omniscient
- Righteous
- Self-existent
- Self-sufficient
- Sovereign
- Transcendent
- Truth
- Wise
- Wrath
- Love
- Mercy

[List compiled at preceptaustin.org from titles of a series of sermons entitled "On the Attributes of God."]

19   My Singing Is a Prayer

Tune: VERMONT
Text: Novella D. Preston Jordan (1901-1991)

"In music, Lord, I worship thee." [3]

This hymn line has probably been the theme of my entire existence… at least back as far as I can remember. I've always found God in music – especially sung music… music with words. I find him most commonly and most profoundly in hymn-singing. That should come as no surprise to those of you who know me well.

I've written several hymn and/or sacred anthem texts over the years. At times, I've tried my hand at writing poems that were not sacred in nature – that did not express anything about my faith: love songs, patriotic songs, country songs – even an opera libretto. I could never seem to make that work because my music – my words – seem to be set aside for worship.

A few years ago, the frenzy over the USA men's team having a tiny shot at winning the World Cup in soccer flooded the airwaves and the print media. One thing I noticed was the incorporation of a rhythmic, highly-repetitive chant: "I be-lieve that we will win! I be-lieve that we will win!" Every sports bar in the country seems to have taken up this "hymn" to the sport of futbol. [More recently, the women's soccer teams have come home with the trophy; but I didn't hear a "hymn" erupt!?]

Historically, when a group shares a common belief, they take up a song to support it. That's why countries have national anthems and patriotic songs – causes have a common song (e.g. "We Shall Overcome") – and religions… all religions I know of… incorporate some form of corporate musical expression into their gatherings.

As you might imagine, I am not caught up in the soccer frenzy, but I am totally committed to expressing my Christian beliefs in song – chiefly the hymns of my faith. That's why I am putting together this book; that's why I created the Old-Fashioned Singing Project; that's why most every Sunday morning with book in hand, I'll be somewhere singing… because "in music, Lord, I find you."

O Worship the King

Tunes: LYONS, HANOVER
Text: Robert Grant (1779-1838)

"Thy bountiful care what tongue can recite?"

In 1985 in the town where I live, THE TRIP TO BOUNTIFUL was filmed. Right here in Waxahachie, Texas, Geraldine Page wandered the streets as Carrie Watts, in search of her fictional hometown: Bountiful. She won an Academy Award for her portrayal... and Cynthia Clawson was nominated for her singing of "Softly and Tenderly."

I never get to this third stanza without recalling that year when all the movie trucks came to town and lined the streets to make Waxahachie looked like Houston in the early 1950's when the action was supposed to have been taking place.

Most of us would like to return to the bountiful care of our childhood... even if our hometown is not called Bountiful. Those days of constant watchful protection: Who can put it into words? According to this hymn-writer, it can't be done. The vastness of God's provision for us is such that it cannot adequately be verbalized. Instead, it is dramatized for us in creation itself:
> It breathes in the air.
> It shines in the light.
> It streams from the hills.
> It descends to the plain.
> It sweetly distills in the dew and the rain.

The generous care of the Holy One works quietly in oxygen and in brightness; it gushes down from the hillside, like a flood rushing through a canyon toward the flatlands; it sweetly lands upon parched places as dew and rainfall. And we stand, awaiting its affects because we are frail, feeble children of dust.

Head back to Bountiful today. Sit on the platform outside the local warehouse. Recall the days gone by, and believe with all certainty that God's bountiful care still abounds!

Come, Holy Spirit, Dove Divine

Common Tune: MARYTON
Text: Adoniram Judson (1788-1850)

"We love your name, we love your laws, and joyfully embrace your cause."

This baptismal hymn was written by the first American missionary to be sent to Burma and stay on the field long enough to establish a faith community. His commission set into motion the great missionary movement from the U.S. to countries around the world. He was passionate about believers' baptism by immersion (as reflected in this hymn) and oversaw the translation of the Bible into the Burmese language. His is a major name among those for whom missions is their cause.

In THIS hymn line, Judson puts the foundation of his calling into our mouths as we sing; and as we repeat them, we speak our own commitment to embrace the cause of Christ… with joy!

There are lots of different Christian causes out there, and around each one there seems to have formed a following. Some of these have morphed into denominations or sects; some have filled gaps in the church's ministry; some have given rise to the greatest movements in church history; others have created division and infighting.

The cause of Christ is to know him and to make him known – to reveal Christ by modeling his life-actions, his attitudes, his sacrificial nature… by anticipating his ultimate reign ("Thy kingdom come…"). When we take up that central cause and avoid the peripheral distractions, we come closer to agreeing with these words when we sing them together.

As mentioned before [see No. 19], every great cause (Christian and otherwise) has incorporated a song. In fact, any time we stand to sing our faith together, we joyfully support the mission of Christ.

Your mission, if you should choose to accept it: Adore his name. Revere his Word. Gladly embrace his cause.

Count Your Blessings

Tune: BLESSINGS
Text: Johnson Oatman, Jr. (1856-1922)

"Do not be discouraged. God is over all."

Frustration and discouragement are two of our most formidable foes, and they often work hand-in-hand. Many times, frustration causes us to expend too much physical energy trying to 'fix' what frustrates us; discouragement consumes our spiritual/mental reservoir.

Elijah was overcome by both when he told God, "I, only I am left" on your side. It's the way Jonah felt as he sat beneath the worm-chewed vine. This is probably how the disciples felt when they needed to feed the five thousand. This is where many of us too often find ourselves.

This simple truth drawn from the last stanza of one of those gospel songs we trip through as if nothing is worth recalling – this truth that "God is over all" is one we are prone to forget, especially on the front-end of discouragement. Eventually – as though slapped up the side of the head – we believing-types will come around to the realization that God is in control, even in overwhelming, exasperating situations.

This does not free us up to do nothing. Instead, it frees us up to move ahead with the blessed assurance that God has it all under control, and we can ease up a little.

I had a minister friend in Denver who in response to his wife's frustration would simply admonish her to "maintain." It was his way of saying "chill out" or "keep your cool." I have at many times brought that word to mind when trying to settle myself down because I fall prey to defeat and discouragement with the best of them!

Maintain your place under God's canopy of oversight. There, may we all find the peace that passes understanding; and in that peace may we WITH GOD work through our frustrating discouragement.

23 God, Whose Purpose Is to Kindle

Common Tunes: EBENEZER, HOLY MANNA
Text: Elton Trueblood (1900-1994)

"Lift the smallness of our vision." [4]

Elton Trueblood was a Quaker theologian, advisor to American Presidents, author, and hymn-writer. This hymn has appeared in many hymnals since its writing in 1966. Because it is in the standard 8.7.8.7.D meter, it has been set to many tunes over the years.

Like Trueblood's powerful voice among American theologians of the 20th Century, this single line jumps out from the hymn text, which is itself a powerful prayer for the church to sing corporately.

It might be said that we are people of great faith but small vision. We verbalize how much we rely on God's leadership and direction, but often we shy away from casting our vision beyond the commonly-held parameters of the world-wide church, our own denomination, our local congregation, or our small circle of Christian friends. No doubt some of the greatest sacred ideas – visions, if you will – have gone by the wayside because the person to whom they were revealed was reluctant to carry them through… to lay them out before others as a viable option for furthering the kingdom. Perhaps they were shared with a few, disparaged (pooh-poohed), and set aside.

I would like to not be considered a person of small faith OR small vision. I'd like to trust the Father's wise bestowment of kingdom plans, and (because they are truly from the Father) run with them with greater vigor. After all, "Where there is no vision, the people (of God) perish." (Proverbs 29:18). And likely, some of us are withering due to our self-imposed limited vision of what God wants to accomplish in our personal lives and in the greater kingdom.

Lord Christ, please lift the smallness of my vision. Amen.

24 Crown Him with Many Crowns

Tune: DIADEMATA
Text: Matthew Bridges (1800-1894)

"Crown him with many crowns…
and hail him as thy matchless King."

I heard a newscaster say, "For a horse to be royalty, it has to wear three crowns." He was, of course, referring to the Triple Crown in horse-racing… a feat most recently achieved by Affirm in 2018.

This hymn's many-crown concept is scriptural (Revelation 19:12), but it is also a 'picture this' image. I understand that in eastern cultures, the official crown of a king was more like a turban, and every time he conquered another kingdom, a piece of cloth in that kingdom's color was wound into the turban. Therefore, the more colored strips in the crown, the more kingdoms he ruled. That is a much easier concept than envisioning a king with several golden crowns stacked on his head!

When we understand this notion, the hymn calls us to give over more and more territory to the Lamb who sits upon the throne – that is, Jesus. That might be submitting more of our personal 'turf' (spiritual growth) or it might summon us to bring more people into the kingdom (evangelism) – or even to reach more world peoples (missions).

Recognizing Christ as our "matchless King" is an important step in our following after him. In worship, we sometimes sing the chorus "There Is None Like You." In this contemporary song, we are echoing this same sentiment: "You are matchless!" We need to revere Christ as the one-and-only truly holy Son of the Most High God. Until we put him in his rightful place, we come up short in our worship.

While the world awaits another Triple Crown champion, the church celebrates the victories of our multi-crowned King – One who was there before the race began and who knows no finish line.

25 Jesus! What a Friend for Sinners

Typical Tune: HYRFYDOL
Text: J. Wilbur Chapman (1859-1918)

"Even when my heart is breaking,
he, my comfort, helps my soul."

Try to wipe Billy Ray Cyrus' "Achy Breaky Heart" out of your mind for a minute, and let's deal with the reality of heartbreak, a dilemma in which we have all found ourselves – maybe many times. It's that feeling that someone has taken each end of your emotional center and wrenched it against itself to the point that it seems to be broken. Always we think it has been damaged beyond repair. Some heartbreak is everlasting. but thankfully, most of the time it is short-lived… even momentary. Either way, for the one who is experiencing the sprain, the feeling is deep and genuine.

Sometimes this injury comes of our own doing; sometimes it is from outside. There are times that we cannot identify the true source or the break, but we know it is happening.

Even then – EVEN THEN Christ is our comfort, helping us bounce back, reviving our soul.

Heartbreak is a difficult thing to discuss with our fellow human confidants. It seems we turn quickly to the One who hears and understands us inside-out. I admit that I have rarely experienced an anguish of this kind that Christ did not come to my aid. Having a little talk with Jesus usually makes it right… at least bearable. It may not repair the relationship or mend the situation… but we DO feel a certain peace or comfort, and we are rewarded with strength for today and bright hope for the next conflict.

Hymns can do so much more for us than songs written for country music clubs. And lines like this one can resonate in our ears just when we need to be reminded that the Christ whose heart was broken more than once can identify with our own despair… and be our comfort.

Even when my heart is breaking… ahhhh.

Hallelujah, what a promise! Hallelujah, what a hope! Hallelujah, what a Savior!

26 Serve the Lord with Gladness

Tune: LEE
Text and Music: B. B. McKinney (1886-1952)

"Listening, ever listening, for the still small voice." [5]

When reading or studying scripture, we often compare ourselves to the characters we encounter there. There are times I identify with Joseph the dreamer or David the musician. I try not to cast my lot with Jacob the deceiver, Judas the betrayer, or Thomas the doubter. Lately, I've felt more like Methuselah!

In my encounters with God, however, I seem to relate more to Elijah than to Paul. I tend to find my richest moments… even guidance for decision-making… in the quieter experiences. Unlike Paul who was struck down in a dramatic on-the-road light show with the booming voice of God questioning his destructive tendencies, I have consistently found God in something that more resembles a still small voice – an inner tugging – a gentle nudge.

In the stillness of the quiet, God's voice I hear.

I'm sure this is why I prefer the more contemplative worship experience to the bombastic… why I yearn for silence in worship – a practice which has slowly been absorbed into constant sound. With Jesus, I sometimes need to "get away from it all" and get myself recentered spiritually.

One of my all-time favorite minister retreats was sponsored by the Cooperative Baptists but held at a convent. Much of our time (including most meals) was spent in total silence. I was invigorated by the absence of instruction, energized by the lack of lecture.

Today's hymn line comes from another one of those rollicking gospel songs familiar mostly to Baptists, I'm afraid. Loping along in 6/8 time, the jig-like melody almost obscures the depth of this tiny phrase:
> *Listening, ever listening, for the still small voice,*
> *His sweet will so precious will be our choice.*

→

If we are going to make it through this life with any degree of success at holiness, we likely need to be constantly (ever) aware of the still small voice of God at work – alert to those directives from deep within – choosing the precious, sweet will of our Lord in order to serve him in gladness. If you are anything like me… if you identify more with Elijah than Paul… that is a must-do assignment.

"Let those who have ears, listen, hear and heed." (Mark 4:9 RGV)

27 Redeemed, How I Love to Proclaim It

Tunes: REDEEMED, ADA
Text: Fanny J. Crosby (1820-1915)

"I sing, for I cannot be silent."

I've never been much of a singer. For someone who loves to sing as much as I do, you'd think I would have been afforded the gift of beautiful vocalization. Fortunately, I had other musical gifts that were applicable to my forty-plus years of music ministry; unfortunately, many congregations expect their music leader to be a top-notch soloist.

As I was growing up, I don't think we sang this hymn; at least, it never registered with me or attached itself to my memory like most of the old songs did. When A. L. (Pete) Butler's setting of this text was published as an anthem in 1967, it became one of my favorites… and years later, he became one of my mentors. His tune has been included in many hymnals since, making it available to congregations to join the singing of this sturdy, well-married tune for the Fanny Crosby text.

For me, I am always drawn to this hymn line: "I sing, for I cannot be silent." I have no choice but to sing… I can't just stand there while the love of Christ is the theme of my song. My lusty, not-so-wonderful raspy baritone voice may draw questioning looks from people down the pew, but that will NOT mute me. I can NOT be silent. I have to sing when the Spirit says "Sing!"

Paul McCartney has a song "Gotta Sing, Gotta Dance." It's not exactly a church song, but it does apply to my discussion. I join him in polishing up my tonsils because I've gotta sing!

While I am all for the sounds of silence in worship; for me as a contemplative, they are imperative to my finding God. Remember, I'm an Elijah-type. I'm sure God enjoys those lengths of absolute breathless silence, but when we rear back and sing – breaking the silence – I imagine a wide smile crosses his face.

That's why I love this hymn. That's why I sing no matter what anyone around me thinks about my intoning talent. "I sing, for I cannot be silent (because) his love is the theme of my song."

Sometimes, you've just gotta!

---

28   Jesus, Lover of My Soul

Typical Tune: MARTYN
Text: Charles Wesley (1707-1788)

"Thou of life, the fountain art.
Freely let me take of thee.
Spring thou up within in my heart."

Okay, it's really three hymn lines today, but they hang together well! It's all about water spraying, drenching and springing up.

We lived in the Kansas City area for a few years in our trek across the country; it seemed God was saying, "Go east, young man." Denver, Kansas City, Chapel Hill. While serving in that great Midwestern city, we learned it is a beautiful town – sort of a hidden jewel. It is nicknamed the City of Fountains; they say it has more fountains than Rome. In the downtown sector, you can literally see a fountain every couple of blocks, especially around their famed Plaza. Not only are most of them spectacular, but they seem to symbolize refreshment! I loved the sound of water splashing – sometimes roaring. They are the life, the fountain art of the city! →

Like most cities, people were forever jumping into the pools beneath the statuary – frolicking about, acting childish, cooling off. Remember the opening of FRIENDS, when the six young adults were acting silly in one of New York's fountains? There is something magnetic about fountains, drawing us into their liveliness… bringing us joy. There is something freeing about taking off your shoes and wading in the effervescence. There is something invigorating about sensing the spray across your face.

Jesus, the lover of my soul is all that (magnetic, freeing, invigorating) and more. He is the original Old Faithful, spouting forth blessings at exactly the right time! He is not only the redeeming fountain filled with blood… he is also the sustaining fountain of life – life!

My relationship with Christ is constantly bubbling up within me, restoring my joy, renewing my outlook, reviving my spirit, bracing my hope.

Notice in these hymn lines the two brief, sincere, implied prayers:
> *"O great Fountain of Life, spring up within my heart. Amen."*
> *"O wonderful Refresher of all souls, let me freely take you in… absorb you. Amen."*

If you don't live in Kansas City, you may not walk past a grand sculpture spewing forth refreshing liquid today; but I encourage you to pray those two short prayers over and over throughout the day… and maybe all your days. Jot them down on a Post-It Note and repeat them to God almost as your mantra* for the day. Let's see if it makes a difference in our outlook and our attitude.

Christ stands with his watering can in hand, ready to pour. Come, stand under the stream. Run through the sprinklers. Have a more-refreshing-than-usual kind of day.

* - a sound, word, or phrase that is repeated by someone who is praying or meditating; a word or phrase that is repeated often or that expresses someone's basic beliefs

Great Is Thy Faithfulness

Tune: FAITHFULNESS
Text: Thomas O. Chisholm (1866-1960)

"Strength for today, bright hope for tomorrow."

This is MY favorite hymn, and this line is so special to me, it won't be that easy to deal with.

From my perspective as one who started going to church nine months before I was born, this hymn line based from Lamentations 3:22-23 sums up what Christ offers those who follow him. There are obviously many other blessings lined up for the taking, but if I have strength for today and bright hope for tomorrow, I can pretty much make it through any day – the ones filled with joy, the ones filled with struggles and sadness, and the ones which just dribble by on an even keel.

Occasionally I hear someone jokingly say, "Lord, give me strength," when they're dealing with problem people... even their children. While it has become a one-off kind of expression, it IS my daily honest desire – my constant prayer. The undergirding of the supportive hand of God is what I seek and what I enjoy. It truly is the gracious gift of strength which has "brought me safe thus far."

Ensconced in my belief system is hope – not just for an eternal resting place or home beyond my dying day. This is a bright hope for the next day... and the next. Sometimes I want to join Annie and sing, "The sun'll come out tomorrow, you can bet your bottom dollar that tomorrow there'll be sun," because I DO believe that a brightness awaits beyond the darkness – after I have laid me down to sleep.

I could pontificate on these two phrases for a long time; however, I will just say that now that I am a child of the King, I would be fine if these two blessings were all I had to go on every day. Fortunately, I am not limited in the number of times and methods these are meted out because God's faithfulness is great, and his mercies are new every morning. Just call me grateful.

→

P.S. – The day I wrote this hymn line, on JEOPARDY! they included a hymns category. When it first came up, I said to Carlita, "I better know all these!" Surely enough, I did. I hope the hymns category will go into their regular rotation for the benefit of us hymn-lovers who are also JEOPARDY! devotees!

30 Praise, My Soul, the King of Heaven

Various Tunes: My Favorite Is ANDREWS
Text: Henry F. Lyte (1793-1847)

"But while mortals rise and perish, God endures unchanging on."

The unchanging nature of God is an attribute to which we should all rally in our worship, our adoration, our reliance… and ultimately, our evangelism. The very fact that the Bible teaches that all else may morph, our God is the great Non-Transformer!

Transformers are great time-consuming toys because you can play with them and change their shape, their function, their appearance, etc. The industry has spawned movies and Saturday morning cartoon series, books, comic books – all offering a fascination with constant change.

However, for me who lives in a world of constant flux, I am delighted that Jehovah is not like that – nor is his Son or his Spirit: these are constantly constant.

Mortals – that is those of us whom God has created and allowed to inhabit this globe for a brief time – we are the ones with all the ups and downs; ours is a roller coaster existence. Just when we think we have made it to the top of our game, we seem to begin some desperate slide. It's true with governments and empires as well as with our created race individually.

I love it when this hymn line comes across the page… and past my lips. I am reminded that God is not only unchanging, but he is also durable. My God has staying power!

Endurance is a great thing in sports, in careers, in ministry, in life in general. Scripture (the book of Revelation in particular) teaches that those who endure to the end shall stand… shall remain standing! So endurance is a good thing for the saints of God. It is sort of like that 'hang in there' philosophy, but there is something more confident implied; with Martin Luther the enduring ones say, "Here I stand. I cannot recant."

Things are probably going to change in my life today. This mortal may undergo several upsurges; there may be plunges involved. In the daily mouse-race, I may win, or I may fall down along the track – tripping on my own feet or being tripped by a fellow racer. There may be societal upheavals that alter my existence. Somewhere in the world, a thriving government may collapse. An unspeakable tragedy may occur. I may need to say today's hymn line to myself as a reminder.

My fixed, ageless, unalterable God will survive, persevere and prevail. He will live on while all else perishes around me. Can I get a hearty "A-men"?

---

31   Wherever He Leads, I'll Go

Tune: FALLS CREEK
Text and Music: B. B. McKinney (1886-1952)

"He drew me closer to his side.
I sought his will to know." [6]

Remember how you were sitting on the couch, and a parent or grandparent sat down beside you, reached over and pulled you snuggly next to them in a seated bear-hug? When you were small, you giggled and hugged back. Perhaps you were told how much you were loved, kissed on the forehead… even given a noogie. As you sat there embraced by someone who truly cared about you, an intimate conversation sometime ensued as you asked, "What was it like when you were growing up? Did you have a dog? Did you really walk a mile-and-a-half to school in knee-deep snow?" Important stuff like that. It's how we got to know our parents and grandparents. →

That's the picture that comes to mind when I sing this hymn line: Jesus reaching over and pulling me toward himself, wrapping his arms around my frame, rubbing me on the head and whispering, "I love you, you know." After I bask in that kind of compassionate expression, I begin to ask him questions – not about dogs and snow, but about what he has in mind for my life.

The image of Jesus drawing me over close to him – that's the one I delight in when I sing this hymn.

Returning to that sofa analogy where I started out: at some point when you were pulled more closely, you may have stiffened and reluctantly returned the affection. It's a shame how we do that. Then some of us became the parent/grandparent pulling a child over closer to us... and cherished those moments – until they began to outgrow their enjoyment thereof. (With fast-maturing grandsons, I can identify with that!)

Over the years, your sofa-time with Jesus may have become less intimate; you may have stiffened and become reluctant to accept these caresses. Remember Jesus said that unless we come to him like a child, we will miss out on the joys of the kingdom.

I know that this next statement of Jesus comes on the heels of some chastisement for the leaders of Jerusalem, but I've always loved how he said, "How often I have longed to gather your children together, as a hen gathers her chicks under her wings." What a pleasant, wonderful thought. However, it is followed by "but you were not willing!" (Luke 13:34)

Let's not be reluctant children of God. Scoot on down the sofa within reach of those strong arms of Jesus. Let him whisper sweet and low. Let him 'love on you' a little today... or a lot! Then ask him what his will is for you – what you should do next for him and the kingdom. It'll warm the cockles* of your heart... and his!

* - Something that warms the cockles of one's heart induces a glow of pleasure, sympathy, affection, or some such similar emotion. What gets warmed is the innermost part of one's being.

Like a River Glorious

Tune: WYE VALLEY
Text: Frances R. Havergal (1836-1879)

"Hidden in the hollow of his blessed hand."

On the security scale, you can't do much better than this! That gigantic, powerful hand of Christ has grasped you, pulled his fingers around you and hidden you from anything outside that might harm you, distract you, or pull you away. You may have heard the phrase "in the grip of grace"; that's what I'm talkin' about when I sing the second stanza of this common-to-most-churches hymn.

We love being held in a place of protection. In fact, when danger lurks, we crawl as far into the palm as we can go, hiding out from anything that might seek to damage or destroy. However, being shielded from distraction is a bit different; when something interesting comes into view through the openings in his fingers – perhaps contrary to the nature of the Father and behavior expected of his children – it is then that we climb up to peer out and survey the possibilities of escape. We lick our lips and rub our hands together, dreaming of what it might be like to go there.

Fortunately for most of us, we pass on the opportunity to vacate the nail-scarred real estate.

In terms of spiritual warfare, the hand of Christ is involved in a tug-of-war every day with forces of evil. Based on what he says to us ["My Father, who gave them me, is greater than all; and no one is able to pluck them out of my Father's hand." John 10:29], all the yanking possible can't win the battle for my soul… for salvation… my relationship.

Swaddled tightly in the sacred grip, I can avoid harm, distraction and abduction. I like it here.

33   Rejoice, Rejoice, Believers

Tune: HAF TRONES LMAPA FARDIG
(Swedish Folk Tune)
Text: Laurentius Laurenti (1660-1722)

"With hearts and hands uplifted, we plead, O Lord, to see the day of earth's redemption that sets your people free."

"Pleading" is a word we use for crying out in desperation. It is an end-of-my-rope kind of crying out – the kind of language we use when we have nowhere else to turn.

In this hymn line, we assume the posture of worship ("with hearts and hands uplifted") to make a distress call to the throne of God, begging for the kind of redemption that sets people free… all people everywhere, whatever their imprisonment.

The Old Testament believers looked forward to a coming monarch who would rule on their behalf and give preference to the people of God. Their awaiting was for an earthly leader… a hero, if you will. We 21st Century Christians are looking forward to the return of Christ; however, we know from Scripture that his leadership style did not include warring and domination. Therefore, we anticipate his grace-filled redemptive advent to (among other actions) unlock various kinds of prison doors.

Carlita and I support a couple of mission efforts whose sole purpose is to free people from enslavement… especially women and children. One of these is International Justice Mission (www.IJM.org). Large non-profit organizations like this are putting feet to desperate pleas for the freedom of others.

At the end of our ropes – perhaps nearing the end of our days, as we await the Second Advent of our Redeemer -- we continue our anxious plea for all who know no freedom, only bondage and oppression, fully believing that this is ONE of the many miracles the Lord Christ will bring in his ever-loving hands when he returns.

Meanwhile, we should be about our Father's business, doing what WE can to see that such cruel persecution might come to an end.

34 Be Still, My Soul

Tune: FINLANDIA (Sibelius)
Hymn: "Be Still, My Soul" – Katharina von Schlegel (1752)

"Leave to your God to order and provide."

Don't you hate to walk up to a machine you need to use and attached to it you find a hand-scrawled, barely legible note that says: "Out of Order"?

Admit it: sometimes our lives are out of order… or are no longer orderly. Things are not where they're supposed to be. Our priorities are out of whack. We may not be able to put our proverbial finger on the problem, but we know it exists.

We seem to understand the provisional nature of God – Jehovah Jireh – the God who provides not only a ram in the thicket to avoid the sacrifice of a Biblical patriarch's child, but also provides for our everyday needs.

We are a little less familiar with the God who wants to order our steps… to lead us not into temptation – not along thorny paths, but rather beside the still waters. God has a plan – a path – in mind for us. He knows what needs to happen in what order for us to have the most abundant life possible. We, on the other hand, want to do things in OUR preferred order, confident that we know what is best for us, forgetting that Our God knows what he is doing.

This hymn line calls us to leave it up to God to perfectly order our lives and to provide exactly what we need… and to do neither based on what we want! That is not nearly as easy as it may sound or as straight-forward as a sugar-coated sermon or devotional might lead us to believe. This kind of turn-it-over performance comes after much rehearsal. Still, it is worth putting forth the effort to achieve this kind of commitment.

Has someone hung a sign on your life that says, "Out of Order"? Leave it up to the original Repairman!

As a reassurance, this stanza ends with this couplet:
> "Be still, my soul, your best, your heavenly Friend
> Through thorny ways leads to a joyful end."

Of the Father's Love Begotten

Tune: DIVINUM MYSTERIUM
Text: Aurelius Clemens Prudentius (384-413)
Translated by John Mason Neale and Henry W. Baker

"To thee, hymn and chant and high thanksgiving and unwearied praises be."

"Oh boy," I hear you saying. "It's time for an ancient plainsong! This hymn has no meter – no beat – no possibility for underscoring by a set-drummer! How can it still be relevant?"

I'll remove my tongue from my cheek and deal with today's hymn line the same way I try to do with all the ones from your favorite hymns and gospel songs.

I managed to survive most of the worship wars during my music ministry. The congregations I served after the war broke out were pretty much committed to staying in the middle of the road; all were traditional in their worship style with some leanings toward the blended – which is so undefinable, I wish it had never been applied to worship! I had to fight a few battles along the way… minor skirmishes, you might say… but I escaped the ravages of war by which so many of my peers were wounded and/or have had their ministries killed off.

I think this text penned within five hundred years of the birth of the Christian church speaks to this in a round-about way, saying that wherever our musical preferences may take us, our praises should be unwearied…fresh, not tired, energized, with sustained enthusiasm, done with vitality.

Some worshipers are 'worn out' by the singing of those old songs their grandmother enjoyed, with too many words and too much deep theology. Some of the rest of us are 'worn down' by trying to keep up with complicated rhythmic songs set to shallow texts projected on screens. Worn out and worn down are the opposite of energized unweariness. Lord, deliver us all!

I am quite sure that God never meant for us to create schisms over musical styles… quite definitely sure. And none of us truly knows what kind of music God prefers in our worship of his Son. What if Gregorian chant is the only one he will accept… or some very ancient Hebrew musical form of which we have no record? Or does he rock out with a driving beat and the screaming of somewhat sacred lyrics? Or is it only when the congregation holds a hymnal and follows the lead of the organ? Does that sound absurd to you? It certainly does to me!

God is listening to our heart-song – There's within my heart a melody! And all of us have to find a congregation whose musical style allows our heart-song to come through with genuine authenticity… not forced, but free… unwearied.

It's obvious from the title of this book where I would fall in most of this if I had to take sides in the worship wars. I've tried really hard to keep my mouth shut and be accepting of all the extremes, while landing somewhere in the middle-- hopefully not 'on the fence' or waffling. I'm pretty firm in where I stand, but I accept that the heart-song of others may require a different outward musical expression.

When you worship in public – whether it be with a stately hymn, un-metered chant, or high-powered amplified thanksgiving – don't let the praise be overshadowed by the music.

Unwearied, vital, energized, fresh, un-encumbered praise of the Most High God. Let it be so!

36 I Need Thee Every Hour

Tune: NEED
Text: Annie S. Hawks (1835-1918)

"Thy promises so rich in me fulfill."

The people who research those sorts of things say that there are over 3,500 promises of God in the Bible. In the New International Version, the word "promise" occurs 69 times... and not once in the Gospels. I found THAT interesting, don't you?

I'm not sure how many promises I would find if I read through the whole of Scripture notating everything that I consider to be a promise of God to his people; I'd be even more confused if I tried to narrow that down to the promises that apply to ME!

I don't need to do that, however, to know that the Word of God is filled with promises and that he has stood behind (or will yet stand behind) everyone he has made. Given my personal understanding of Jehovah God, he wouldn't 'waste his breath' on any promise if it were not significant... important... or as this hymn line says *rich*.

I looked up the word "rich" in Webster's and found a lot of synonyms which apply to the promises of God: abundant, of high value or quality, well-supplied, magnificently impressive, highly productive, full of nutrients, pure. Annie Hawks may not have turned to Webster when she wrote this text, but having dissected the word, I think she selected the perfect word to describe the promises and blessings of God.

Fulfill means to complete or carry out. I've always thought of it as being filled-full... to the point of overflowing. In this case, I think that applies and makes the prayer-line even more powerful. I guess I want to not only be standing on the promises; I want to be drowning in them!

Simply put, may this be our prayer today: *Let your rich promises be realized in my life. Amen.*

P. S. – As is the case in so many hymns, this hymn line is tucked into stanza three – the one we too often skip… the one rich with truth that is often stolen from those of us who worship. Let's add a new commandment for worship-planners: "Thou shalt not steal a stanza from any hymn that thou shalt sing with thy thinking congregants, especially the third."

---

37   Lift High the Cross

Tune: CRUCIFER
Text: George W. Kitchin (1827-1912)

"So shall our song of triumph ever be:
Praise to the Crucified for victory!"

This is not a hymn I grew up singing. The first time I sang it at a Chorister's Guild event, it burned a place deep in my memory; it is a moment I'll never forget. "What a wonderful hymn," I whispered to myself as the tall brass cross was carried down the aisle at some church in north Dallas where the conference was being held. Every time we hit the refrain, a new part of my faith soared: "Lift high the cross. The love of Christ proclaim till all the world adore his sacred name."

The stanzas of this hymn are very brief. Today's hymn line is an entire stanza… usually printed as the last. It sums up the gist of the entire hymn: Therefore, our everlasting song of praise will be to the One who was crucified – whose victory over death and the grave allowed us to triumph as well. HIS victory has given US a song of triumph.

So sing it, sister!

38   I Will Sing the Wondrous Story

Tunes: WONDROUS STORY, HYFRYDOL
Text: Francis H. Rowley (1854-1952)

"(Jesus) threw his loving arms around me, drew me back into his way."

This hymn line picks up on the Good Shepherd image:
I was lost, but Jesus found me,
Found the sheep that went astray,
Threw his loving arms around me,
Drew me back into his way.

A stray lamb: that would describe most of us at one time or another... maybe now. We've wandered off from the fold and find ourselves lost and alone – maybe wet and cold – for sure, miserable. We may have moseyed off accidentally, made a wrong turn, suddenly realized we were detached from the flock. Others of us may have found ourselves in this condition because we made an attempt to escape; we were like the prodigal. Perhaps we felt forced out because we didn't fit in anymore. Whatever the reason, we are aware that we are strays.

The beauty of the Good Shepherd analogy is this: we are find-able.

The Ever-searching One cleans us up, dries us off, throws a blanket around us to be sure we are warm, feeds our hunger, makes sure we are well again and that we find our way "back into his way."

Even as a young child, this stanza of the hymn caught my attention and seared into my brain the beauty of the picture it painted... long before I knew the John 10 passage or appreciated the great artworks based on the metaphor.

The next time we are estranged, let's try this hymn/prayer:
I am lost. Jesus, find me.
Find this sheep who's gone astray.
Throw your loving arms around me,
Draw me back into your way.

Open My Eyes That I May See

Tune: SCOTT
Text & Music Clara H. Scott

"Silently now I wait for thee, ready."

I may have learned this hymn at Vacation Bible School in the late 50's. In straight lines reaching all the way to the main street through Pigeon Forge – a thoroughfare much less-traveled than it is today - we followed the flags and the Bible into the cavernous sanctuary to make our way through two weeks of intense Bible study and craft-making. (Editorially speaking: most churches here had a four-day VBS this past summer.) That may have been the year I got the pole of the American flag caught in my open fly at commencement ceremonies, but that's a story for later, I'm sure.

I have very fond memories of my summer weeks spent at VBS. That's where I learned the order of the books of the Bible and where I memorized some of my life verses. Many summers my Mama taught at another church out in the country, so I did four weeks… and ended up with a double set of crafts! The order of the Bible books remained the same, however.

This hymn line from the refrain of "Open My Eyes That I May See" has three out-standing words – silently, ready and waiting – all of which speak to us more as adults than they did as young learners; their impact on our mind development and spiritual formation is probably more profound than any of us imagine or would dare admit.

Ready and waiting in silence: that's how we say we are positioned to receive direction from the One who trends our path. We find ourselves at the corner of Ready and Waiting… at least that's what we 'say'! I must admit that many times I am waiting to hear from God, but I am not always ready to accept the instructions with which I am charged. My guess is that if you are honest, you are that way, too.

In my early years in the music ministry, I remember how mercilessly we ribbed a girl in the youth choir because she literally lived at the corner of Willing and Waiting! Fortunately, she took it well, waited

→

until the right guy came along (from within the youth group) and has lived happily ever after.

However, standing at various crossroads in our lives, decision-making is not easy until we are ready and waiting… or willing and waiting! That is where I sincerely want to stand in my relationship to God's call, because when those two are aligned, obedience will follow naturally.

I'm pushing my contemplative button here, but I'm convinced that the only time we clearly hear is when we are quiet – silent – still. Our in-constant-motion lives and our air-filled-with-noise waking hours impede God's ability to speak a loud and clear message… to give distinct direction to our wandering feet – ready and willing though they may be.

> *Silently now I wait for thee.*
> *Ready, my God, thy will to see.*
> *Open my eyes.*
> *Illumine me, Spirit Divine.*

Go to the corner of Ready and Waiting. Wait silently. Do not pass go or try to collect $200! Stay there as long as needed. Repeat as often as necessary.

---

40   Joyful, Joyful, We Adore Thee

Tune: HYMN TO JOY
Text: Henry van Dyke (1852-1933)

"Wellspring of the joy of living"

Ever been to a "well house" or a "spring house"? One of the perks of growing up in the country is having experiences that just not everybody has enjoyed, and this may well be one of them for me.

My mother took us – I should say dragged us – annually to the place where she was born: a then unoccupied, tumbled-down structure sitting amongst several acres of weeds. Each time we visited that plot of ground, the house was more tumbled-down than the previous year. I never liked walking through the weeds for fear of snakes and other east Tennessee varmints, but we trudged from the road toward the spot so dear to the childhood of Hedy Inez Smelcer Huff.

Although the house was dilapidated and was eventually razed, there still stood the well house. It was terribly small, built of some earthy substance kind of like adobe... my Dad called them mud bricks... with a wood shingled roof. This tiny structure was built over a spring – an artesian well. That fresh-water source was so important to the families who had lived there originally that they covered it. I understand that it was always cool in there, so they sort of used it as a refrigerator, too.

On the outside of the well house there hung a tin dipper. After all those years, the dipper still hung there. And without thought of who may have used the dipper last, we always carried it inside and had a drink of the amazingly cold, fresh water. Perrier had nothing on this natural spring! And if you've never drunk from a tin dipper, you don't understand the sensation - the rush - when the cold tin hits your lips before the water does. I can still remember it as if it were yesterday although it was well over fifty years ago. That annual trek to the well house was one of the memorable joys of my growing up years.

Therefore, every time I sing this hymn line, I'm reminded of the ice-cold tin dipper filled with water. And without thought of the unsanitary way we participated in the rich history of that long-flowing spring, I realize once again that God is truly like that spring: still there, still available, still refreshing those who drink of him. All I have to do is dip into the well and enjoy.

PS - When my grandmother Charity Smelcer died, the only one of her possessions I requested was the tin dipper that always rested on the counter by her kitchen sink -- used daily by her and all the rest of us in the family. Who needed a Dixie cup when you could drink from a common cup? It's pretty beat up, but it hangs by the door that leads to our garage, reminding me every morning of my roots... and the taste of cold well water.

41   **Jesus, Keep Me Near the Cross**

Tune: NEAR THE CROSS
Text: Fanny J. Crosby (1820-1915)

"Near the cross, O Lamb of God,
bring its scenes before me."

It is difficult for most of us to think on the extreme suffering of Christ during those last hours – the scourgings, the pressing down of the thorns into his forehead, the struggling through the streets of Jerusalem beneath the cross-bar, the nailing of his hands and feet to the cross, the piercing of his side, his final breath. Just typing those phrases was not a pleasant experience.

I remember when Mel Gibson's THE PASSION OF THE CHRIST hit the screens, many fine Christians refused to go because it was so gruesome; they did not want to see such a graphic reenactment. The church I served at the time in Chapel Hill rented the theater across the street, watched it together, and came back to the church for the pastor to unpack it for us.

Everything about the faith-life doesn't need to be pleasant. I certainly did not "enjoy" that film, but my understanding of the suffering Servant was strengthened by the experience.

This third stanza (often skipped in congregational singing) is the only one in which Fanny Crosby addresses Christ directly; it is in fact a brief prayer:

> Near the cross, O Lamb of God, bring its scenes before me.
> Help me walk from day to day with its shadow o'er me.

In our process of understanding the cross-event, it is necessary that we not look away… that we not turn our eyes away from Jesus. With Miss Crosby, we need to ask that the scene be played over and over in our mind's eye. This act of replaying might well help us walk more closely to our Savior, as the beautiful awfulness of the cross casts an eternal shadow across our earthly pathway.

Note: This was my mother's favorite hymn.

42 Beneath the Cross of Jesus

Tune: ST. CHRISTOPHER
Text: Elizabeth Clephane (1830-1869)

"Beneath the cross of Jesus, I gladly take my stand."

Following the previous hymn line about proximity to the cross, this opening phrase from one of my favorite Lenten hymns has a similar theme. After this statement of our "place" <u>beneath</u> the cross, we are drawn within "the shadow of a mighty rock" described as "a home within the wilderness, a rest upon the way."

We often steer away from singing this hymn because in the original text printed in most hymnals, the word "fain" is used instead of the word "gladly." When our mind has to stop and wonder what a word means, we sometimes lose the thought that follows; therefore, I'm glad that some books and arrangements are using less archaic language to help us 'get it' without explanation!

I would have used the word "proudly," but pride is such a no-no in church-speak! However, we should be proud to take our stand with Christ at the foot of his cross, shouldn't we?!

Taking our stand <u>for</u> Christ and <u>with</u> Christ is vital for those of us who would be counted as one of His. Our placement keeps people from second-guessing who we are and whose we are. In today's society, that establishment of our post is key to our vitality as witnesses to "the very dying form of One who suffered there for me."

Looking for prime real estate in the Kingdom? Find it beneath the cross of Jesus.

43 Eternal God, May We Be Free

Tune: CANONBURY
Text: Michael G. Dell (1959-   )

"From worship that is insincere with shallow words and thoughtless prayer may we be free." [7]

This hymn line written by somebody ten years younger than I is so on-target, it makes me shudder! And if you happen to read this on a Sunday morning before you head to church, it is a particularly poignant prayer. I'm not sure it appears in any book other than The Baptist Hymnal 1991, but it should!

In the worship war discussion, the one thing that comes to the surface most often is authenticity of those who plan and lead worship – whatever the musical style – whether contemporary or liturgical – whether dancing the aisles or standing and kneeling. Therefore, this request of God that our worship be sincere is exactly where we should always begin. I probably took most everything about my music ministry pretty seriously, but when it came to worship planning and implementing, I was about as sincere as they come.

Shallow words. Hmmm. When selecting hymns and anthems, I always look first at the text; then I move on to see how the music sounds against the text. I realize that I don't want to put anything in the mouth of a worshiper that they don't believe or shouldn't believe. In my humble opinion, fluff and filler just have no place in worship-singing. For sure, if the text is too deep to get your mind around, it won't work in the corporate setting; those are more likely to minister to us as devotional literature when we have more time to reflect on the depth. Dr. Louis Ball taught me over the years that the congregation should be able to grasp the basic meaning of the text the first time they sing it—subtleties later.

The last thing Dell encourages us to stay away from is thoughtless prayer. Our conversation with God (whether aloud or silent) should not be throw-away moments. Like the rest of our worship, the prayers should not be insincere or shallow. I personally prefer to write out my public prayers when I'm called upon to lead in worship; maybe that's why I'm rarely invited to do so! Rambling, rote... yea even thoughtless are not the kinds of prayers I want to lift-up in worship... or the kind I want to hear!

So, do you think I am prejudiced toward this hymn line? You're dang right, I am! This should be the prayer of all of us who congregate to participate in the highest hour of the Christian week – whatever the worship style. I hope against all hope that those who put the services together have already approached their job with this kind of prayer.

Insincere, shallow, thoughtless – not good worship words, wouldn't you agree? Go thou and do un-likewise!

---

44   He Leadeth Me

Tune: HE LEADETH ME
Text: Joseph H. Gilmore (1834-1918)

"Lord, I would clasp my hand in thine,
nor ever murmur or repine,
content whatever lot I see."

We're sort of back to that 'and he walks with me and he talks with me' kind of hymn, but I picture this one to be more like a child who grabs ahold of an adult's hand, fully believing there is safety in that grasp. Walking hand-in-hand with the Savior is something we all aspire to ... shoulder-to-shoulder in locked step, going only where his trajectory leads.

Picture this, if you will: The Lord Jesus extends his hand and looks you in the eye. You're invited to place your hand in that nail-scarred hand, but you are not forced to accept the gesture – you don't even feel obligated. But you clasp your palm into his, and you feel the sudden strong squeeze that reassures you that you have made the right move. Although we may visualize the two of you walking together, that may not happen; he may just stand there with you – perfectly still in the midst of chaos. Sometimes that's what we need: not necessarily a walking buddy but a standing companion. "Just hold my hand while I

→

work my way through this situation," might be our request – sort of like, "All I need is a hug."

I get "into" this hymn line every time I sing it, and I've been singing it most of my life – since my earliest memories of congregational singing in the white wood-frame church that was Pigeon Forge Baptist Church before we moved over into the big brick building on the parkway.

I love to imagine hanging on for dear life to the hand of my Lord the Christ. And I like promising him that I won't complain about my life – that I'll be content in whatever state I find myself... even Texas!

It is not an easy promise to make, because we seem to need to vent our frustrations and our unhappinesses. But unlike a recent best-seller, I have never been disappointed with God. I have been disappointed with my own decisions and mistakes. I have been disappointed by God's people. But I have never been disappointed with God. And despite having sung this promise for over sixty years now, I have occasionally complained to God about my situation and have not always been as contented as Elsie.

It is still my intention. It is still my prayer, because this hymn line concludes with "content whatever lot I see, since 'tis thy hand that leadeth me." 'Tis still his hand... and sometimes he has to squeeze a little harder to remind me of my promises and my commitments to him and to his Kingdom.

45 It Is Well with My Soul

Tune: VILLE DU HAVRE
Text: Horatio Spafford (1828-1888)

***"My sin, not in part, but the whole
is nailed to the cross, and I bear it no more."***

This is a favorite hymn of many… and it is way up the favorite chart at the Huff house. When I was at Southwestern Seminary and they still sang hymns in chapel, they did a survey of favorite hymns of students, placing this one at the top, just above "To God Be the Glory" and (of course) "Amazing Grace"!

Sadly, this is the stanza (the to-be-most-pitied third) often skipped over when one is jettisoned for time purposes in worship-planning. I say "sadly" because after the flowing of peaceful rivers, sorrows rolling like sea-billows, Satan buffeting, and the coming of great trials, THIS stanza tells why it is well with my soul.

Some hymn lines I just can't sing aloud; I get choked up, teared up… and I just mouth the text. This is one of those. Spafford has worded for me what I could not say on my own: all my sin – not just part, but the whole of it – has been nailed to the cross along with my Redeemer. As one who has trouble letting go, this line reminds me that I can release it; I no longer have to shoulder my transgressions. Sometimes when I am given opportunity to sing this stanza, I gather my wits and am able to phonate by "Praise the Lord, O my soul!"

Sometimes in worship or in a retreat setting, we are given opportunity to scribble some iniquity on a 3" x 5" card and symbolically lay it at the foot of the cross… or even tack it to a wooden facsimile. It's a nice little exercise, but it can only be fully understood if you bring at least three packages of cards with you… and then use both sides! It's that "sin, not in part, but the whole" that completes the imagery.

I'm a Kenny Chesney fan. Sorry, musical-snob friends, it's true! He has a great song called "There Goes My Life." You can Google it later. But for now, each time you pass a wooden cross on display, smile a little bit and say with all kinds of sincere confidence, "There goes my sin… all of it."

46 Dear Lord and Father of Mankind

Common Tunes: REST (sometimes called ELTON), and REPTON
Text: John Greenleaf Whittier (1807-1892)

"In deeper reverence, praise."

I love that many great poets – critically acclaimed, highly respected among literature scholars – wrote some meaningful poetic expressions of their Christian faith… and that some of those have been set to music, like this one.

The four-word phrase I've chosen for this hymn line is the ending of the first stanza. In context, it reads like this:
In purer lives thy service find, in deeper reverence, praise.

From pure motives may our service emerge. In the depth of reverence may we express our praise. What wonderful objectives for those of us who seek nearness to the heart of God.

Reverence is becoming a rarely-practiced art. The noise of our worship doesn't allow for that centering of our quiet self on "the depths of the riches both of the wisdom and knowledge of God." (from Romans 11:33) Instead, the ecstatic joy of the Lord has become our strength.

Every now and then, though, the most exuberant worshiper has a strong craving to find the deeper reverence of solitude, one-on-One with the holy God… to be still and know for sure that God IS God.

Surface faith is nearly worthless. When the commitment and the submission are epidermic, it does little good… for the person or the kingdom.

O that we might in awe search out the depths of our faith experience – that we might be astonished at what we discover as the Almighty is quietly venerated. In the noiselessness, we might hear the still small voice more clearly and come away refreshed by the praise we render in the soundproof room of the soul.

47 In Heavenly Love Abiding

Various Tunes – most common in the U.S. is NYLAND
Text: Anna L Waring (1820-1910)

"In heavenly love abiding,
no change my heart shall fear."

This is my wife Carlita's favorite hymn, and it opens with these phrases:
In heavenly love abiding, no change my heart shall fear;
For safe is such confiding, for nothing changes here.

It's a hymn about spiritual stability. When surrounded by and supported by the deep, deep love of Jesus, no matter how many storms rage about us, we have no reason to fear. There is a certain safety factor which is unsurpassed by any other shelter in the time of storm.

Our lives go through so many changes. Every paradigm seems to be shifting – and some of those paradigms have been our way of life, way of worship, way of doing things for all our years. But even when caught up in the squall of constant adjustments, we can be confident that this love of God has not and will not change… and neither will our relationship with God.

We can abide confidently in him as he abides in us… as branches – offshoots – of who God is, producing fruit in every season, even the tempestuous ones.

Lots of public buildings now have a sign on the outside that reads "Safety Zone." Those have been designated for people who are living their lives in fear of someone who may want to do them harm. We all desire a place we can count on – a hiding place. For those of us who seek him, God becomes for us that kind of refuge… our safety zone.

Stop running away from your troubles; run instead toward that safe place, near to the heart of God.

And the final stanza gives us even further confidence:
My life I cannot measure, the path of life is free.
My Savior has my treasure, and he will walk with me.

Footsteps of Jesus

Tune: FOOTSTEPS
Text: Mary B. Slade (1826-1882)

"We will rest where the steps of Jesus end at his throne."

The first Sunday in June, they celebrate "Decoration Day" in my hometown, an annual tradition common to rural areas in some southern states. Many of you who read this will be unfamiliar with the ritual of decorating the graves of the departed, but to many folks, this is a big deal. The hillside in Pigeon Forge, Tennessee, where my parents, grandparents and other family saints are buried is at its most colorful of the year – adorned with bouquets great and small… real flowers, plastic and silk reproductions. It becomes for most a reunion day – the only time on the calendar when they come into contact with old friends and family members.

These whose lives are remembered on that weekend are those who have entered their eternal rest – whose pathways in their earthly life were intent on following the footsteps of Jesus wherever they might have been steered. Their proximity to the feet of Jesus would obviously bring them to sit at his feet as he sits now enthroned.

Many of those who've gone on before us into glory had rough, difficult lives, surviving the Great Depression, World Wars, years of un-productive crops and/or dying livestock, factory shut-downs and lay-offs, and so on. They rarely found time to slow down and rest. Most knew nothing of vacations or getting away for a weekend; many had never ventured outside their county or state.

Their pastors may have in their sermons painted glorious pictures of the pearly gates opening into ivory palaces with streets paved with gold; but for most of the bedraggled listeners in the pew, their ears perked up when there was mention of the promised rest. Not only would they meet their loved ones there, but they would actually have time to fellowship with them for extended periods of time without being bothered by animal feedings, seed-planting/harvesting or punching a time clock… or taking care of an extended family's needs.

Let's admit it: We, too, look forward to heaven's rest more than we look forward to the architecture.

Either way, it behooves us to follow in the steps of Jesus so that when we arrive at the throne, we'll recognize his nail-scarred feet – then we can lift our eyes to behold him face to face. We'll spend time praising him; we'll catch up with those who got there before us and know their way around. And the rest (remainder) will be rest.

---

49   Rock of Ages, Cleft for Me

Tune: TOPLADY
Text: Augustus M. Toplady (1740-1778)

"In my hand no price I bring; simply to thy cross I cling."

At the end of each summer, on television I watch stories of lesser-fortunate parents standing in line to receive free school supplies and required vaccinations for their children. After some great disaster hits (natural or otherwise), we have observed long lines of displaced individuals awaiting food, clothing and necessities. I remember driving past city missions with homeless men cued up for blocks anticipating the opening of the doors so they could get in from the cold for a good hot meal and a warm place to spend the night.

In every one of these cases, as the line moves forward and the people receive that for which they have come to these places, no cashier is standing at the end of the line expecting to be paid. No paperwork may even be required; they are simply provided with what they came for.

This is how you and I have been graced by God. When we have arrived at the serving table, we may have made some vain attempt to pay for the bundle he has prepared for us, but he gladly hands us his great salvation. We fumble for our wallet; he grabs our hand and says, "No charge."

Somehow, we are not comfortable with the free gift of salvation; we WANT to pay for it ourselves; we don't want a hand-out; we NEED to work for it or pay it off a little at a time. In our protesting, God may

→

be a bit offended because he's trying his best to give us a free gift, and we insist on making some kind of payment.

In that long line of sinners poor and needy, you and I have arrived face to face with the One in charge of distribution. With no price in hand, we accept the free gifts of God's grace simply because the cross stands bare, the tomb stands empty, the throne stands occupied. Love's redeeming work is done. We move aside as another weary soul comes to the front of the line; without personal payment, they too walk away with what they have come for.

Know somebody who needs to be in that line? Do they need someone to stand with them? Are they confused about the no-payment-necessary part of the transaction? Help them understand. Tell them how it works. Joy with them when they receive what they come seeking.

Put your wallet away. Stop trying to figure out a long-term payoff plan. Even if you try, you can't afford it. Jesus paid it all. Now move out of the way and let somebody else enjoy the same blessing.

---

50   Come, Thou Fount of Every Blessing

Tunes: NETTLETON, WARRENTON
Text: Robert Robinson (1735-1790)

"Tune my heart to sing thy grace."

I had an aunt in Tennessee who played a great "country piano". She could add all those runs and flourishes that make the Saturday-night-singing southern style work so well. I'm not sure she could read a note of written music, but she could make any familiar gospel song come to life.

In an unheated, non-air conditioned room in her farm house she played the heck out of that piano for a while most every day, but she never had the piano tuned. Over the years, the tuning got so bad, there was no longer an identifiable pitch to any key; there were 88 out-of-tune notes on her piano. Little by little, she didn't even notice. To the rest of us, her playing was a blurred smear of noise; as far as she was concerned, she still heard the melodies and harmonies. It's sort of like that hackneyed illustration of the frog in the boiling water pot – as the tuning went away, my aunt lost all her sense of musical hearing.

I vividly remember being at her house on a Christmas Eve when she began to play what I thought must have been a carol. Turning to me she said, "Go ahead. Sing, Ronald George!" I had no earthly idea what she was playing; I knew the meter was grouped in two's, but beyond that, I recognized nothing! My reply, "I don't think I know that one," was to no avail. "Everybody knows, 'Joy to the World'," she said. So I broke into an atonal singing of the carol as whole-heartedly – and with as little internal laughter – as I could!

Have you ever been in a room when someone was tuning a piano? It is not an easy process to endure. Tuners are highly-skilled and trained in what is becoming a lost art, and how THEY stand it, I'll never know. But it is something that just has to be done if we are to hear the notes with any clarity.

Sometimes, my heart gets out of tune. Like my Baldwin grand, I need a good tuning; like my Toyota Rav4, I need a tune-up. That's when my hymn-filled brain turns to this hymn line, and I ask God to tune my heart so I can better express his gracious self.

Like piano-tuning, it may not be an easy process to endure, but it is something that must be done occasionally if those around me are to hear the gospel lived out through me.

Things to do today: call a piano technician, schedule a mechanic, get my life back in tune.

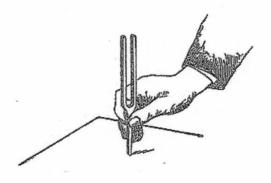

Breathe on Me

Tune: TRUETT
Text: Edwin Hatch (1835-1889)
Adapted and set to music by B. B. McKinney (1886-1952)

"My stubborn will subdue."

A few years ago there was a very popular book published by James Dobson called THE STRONG-WILLED CHILD. People in my church were discussing it almost as if it should be added to the canon. It seems that every parent in the country began to think that they had the one about which he was writing. I never read it because at the time all my 'children' were those in my choirs at the church… and in my opinion most of them were plenty strong-willed!

The book would not have been nearly as marketable as "The Stubborn Child," but that's basically what Dobson was trying to help parents deal with.

Our heavenly parent must feel the same way about us… his stubborn children! Don't you wonder if God has a shelf full of books on how to deal with his children? Of course, he doesn't – he's all-knowing, you know! But my guess is that there are times when he gets pretty frustrated with us when we dig in our heels, stomp our feet, bang our hands on the floor and scream loudly… figuratively speaking, of course. The truth is, most of us can be stubborn at times; even as adults, our strong-willed child rises to the surface.

In this hymn line, we pray an incredibly poignant prayer when we ask God to mollify the part of us which tends to be rebelliously determined… even obstinate. The picture of a horse being reined in comes to my mind – those scenes we've seen in movies where the wildest breeds of horse are in the corral, and they are being brought under the control of the one in charge until finally they are almost docile – even useful.

Okay, Lord Jesus: by the breath of your Spirit calm my restlessness, my inflexible insubordinate self in order that I may be useful-er – make that more useful – to you, to your kingdom, and to the world in which I have been placed. *Take thou my heart, cleanse every part…* including my stubborn streak! Amen.

The Master Hath Come

Tune: ASH GROVE
Text: Sarah Doudney (1841-1926)

***"The Master hath called us in life's early morning
with spirits as fresh as the dew on the sod."***

I learned "The Ash Grove" at Pigeon Forge Elementary School in Mrs. Hester's class… back when school children sang together every day. We didn't have music education as such, but we had a song book provided by some local businesses – and they passed them out every morning, and we sang from them. I have always loved the rise and fall of the waltz-y Welsh melody and was eventually pleasantly surprised to find out it was also a hymn tune!

Most days, I'm a morning person. I like to climb out of bed and get my day started. There is just something re-invigorating about the possibility of starting over… of hitting a 'reset' button and trying to do better this day than any previous day: to accomplish more with my tasks, be more creative with my output, and be more Christ-like in my human interactions.

As a hymnwriter myself, I know that there are blessed few words that rhyme with God. Doudney could have talked about dew that was fresh on the grass or the ground, but she was headed toward "the people of God," so her choices were limited!

Fresh spirits – refreshed spirits – to begin every early morning: the Master has called us to face each day from its first moments with a sense of starting over because we have been graced with possibilities to improve… to be our best.

My favorite song from JESUS CHRIST SUPERSTAR is the final chorus as the cast sings "Could We Start Again Please?" It applies to today's hymn line, and, based on the biblical account of the nature of God, the answer is an emphatic "Yes! Start again with spirits as fresh as the dew on the sod!"

O blessed Restarter of all lives halted, Recharger of all spirits drained – do a wonder in my life this morning that I might make the very most of this day. Amen.

In Loving-Kindness Jesus Came

Tune: HE LIFTED ME
Text & Music: Charles H. Gabriel (1856-1932)

*"When I took him at his word,
forgiven he lifted me."*

The title of this hymn (the first line) sends out a strong message about the way Jesus came… and continues to enter… our struggling world: in a kindness based out of love – an intense affection only possible through the power of God at work in his life. It's an image of the Son of God gently making his entrance among his people. He did not barge in and take over with fanfare or bombast. So far as we know from his Word, everything about him was kind, intentional, filled with grace and truth.

If we take him at his word (or Word), we find him willing and able to redeem us. Questioning is not a bad thing; it is in fact a healthy faith exercise. Doubt on the other hand… not so much. The opposite of taking him at his word is doubting the core of his message… disbelieving that he can work a miracle in our lives.

My dad, Raymond, was known to be a man of his word. In my earliest years I recall his making land deals and buying cars with a down-payment and a handshake. He got burned a few times, but as far as I know, he never went back on his word.

The Lord Christ was and is known to be a Man of his word. In our case, he has accepted our admission of estrangement, and in place of a handshake has handed us forgiveness for those actions and attitudes which have separated us from his holiness. And the best news is that he does this for us every day: he has promised to keep on forgiving us – we have his word on that.

Need a lift? Yeah, me too. Let's take him at his word, accept his loving, kind forgiveness, and be elevated by tender hand from sinking sand. When it's all said and done, we can sing, "O praise his name! He lifted me."

At Calvary

Tune: CALVARY
Text: William R. Newell (1868-1956)

"Mercy there was great, and grace was free. *
Pardon there was multiplied to me.
There my burdened soul found liberty."

The "there" in these three phrases is "At Calvary," the title of the hymn.

I am very fond of the mercy of God. I've said that before, and I'll likely say it again. I may have been an adult before I realized that the words mercy and grace are interchangeable. When you grow up in Sunday School, you learn the list of words – the Christian vocabulary – but you don't always get the meaning of each one… at least not enough to compare them with one another. It was, however, a good day when that light bulb went off.

With maturity, I began to appreciate the notion of grace and/or mercy. When it occurred to me that one cannot be a person of grace and be judgmental at the same time, it truly revolutionized my Christian life. When you grow up with an implied "us and them" mentality, judgmentalism just comes naturally. We never stood and sang together, "Let's take the role of judge for those who disagree with us." (That works to the ELLACOMBE tune, by the way!) But we often sang hymns about mercy and grace… like the one cited here today. To my young – dare I say "rebellious" spirit – I felt like we were not living out the message of some of our favorite hymns and gospel songs.

Whenever I'm called upon to elaborate (or devotionalize) on mercy, I quote these three phrases from the refrain of this hymn. It tells us
1) The mercy of God is huge.
2) The grace of God is a free gift.
3) The pardon (forgiveness) of God was distributed exponentially.
4) The liberating power of God unburdens… unchains.

I've even quoted this hymn at weddings, encouraging couples to commit to treating one another with great grace in their union.   →

The next time you need a lift in your day, say (or sing) this chorus over to yourself. Unless you're just tied down in overwhelming judgementalism, it will be a total refreshment to your soul.

Or the next time you feel a hypercritical, disapproving urge coming on, start humming these truths from the hymnal; see if you don't find them to head you more toward Christlikeness and further away from that person you might easily become.

> * - I sometimes think this means that at the cross-event, the grace of God was loosed… set free to act as an agent of salvation and reconciliation. That's probably a stretch, but if the phrase were "… and grace was freed," it would make perfectly good sense. Either way, I think that IS what happened.

---

55   He Giveth More Grace

Tune: HE GIVETH MORE GRACE
Text: Annie Johnson Flint (1866-1932)

"When we reach the end of our hoarded resources, our Father's full giving is only begun."

Written by a schoolteacher whose career was cut short by crippling arthritis, this stands as her only still-sung hymn. In fact, it was popularly sung as a solo in the 1940's and 50's and has only recently been included in books for congregational use.

In a very poetic way, Flint was able to capture FDR's "when you come to the end of your rope, tie a knot and hang on" adage in a way which beautifully depicts the abundant generosity of God.

When we have tried in our own strength to accomplish great tasks or to overcome great difficulties, we can "tie a knot" in our rope and wait for God to intervene.

To put this hymn line in context, here is the full stanza:
> *When we have exhausted our store of endurance,*
> *When our strength has failed when the day is half-done,*
> *When we reach the end of our hoarded resources,*
> *Our Father's full giving is only begun.*

We all know that we should have sought out his assistance and guidance in the first place, but our human nature has caused us to turn to some other colloquial adages like "pull yourself up by your bootstraps" and "I did it my way!" We join the chugging uphill steam engine repeating the mantra "I think I can! I think I can!" We have yet again been Oprah-ized into self success.

Over my 70 years, I have accumulated a good number of creative resources; I've had to reason my way through many dilemmas in my ministry and my personal life. Amazingly, sometimes that works for me. Other times, I come up way short on my "hoarded resources" and have to send out my call for help. I'm not alone in this; I have many cohorts in this method of doing life!

I love the way Flint calls God's openhandedness "full giving"... and that we only see the tip of that generosity: It is only beginning to kick in on our behalf.

I would dare say that everyone reading this hymn line today is approaching the end of their rope in some area of their life-journey – and as far as you can tell, the end of that rope is nearing more rapidly than we would like to admit. Go ahead and tie that proverbial knot and wait; stop trying to achieve success on your own. Allow God's full-giving nature to activate itself in your situation. See if the burden isn't lifted... or at least lessened.

---

56   Nearer, My God to Thee

Tune: BETHANY
Text: Sarah F. Adams (1805-1848)

"Still all my song shall be: Nearer, my God, to thee."

It is a real shame that this hymn is mostly remembered as what the band was playing when the Titanic went down and is typically relegated to memorial services and funerals. The haunting, usually-slowly-sung hymn has some wonderful brief phrases worth recounting. It speaks of steps leading into heaven, angels beckoning

→

us homeward, thoughts brightened with praise… and references to the Jacob's ladder-dream (Genesis 28:12).

My outstanding word in this hymn line for today is "still." It's a great word we use when we mean "after all this time." I suppose that's one of the reasons it is associated with funerals or end-of-life events.

Job uses this word many times in his defense against those who encourage him to turn from his God, such as in chapter 13, verse 15: "Though he take away my life, still will I hope in him." (Some translations use the word 'yet,' meaning the same as 'still.')

It is that kind of continuing steadfastness to which we all aspire – those of us who seek to be faithful followers of the Lamb. It is our intention to come to the end of our days, still using the word "still"! Of course, you know that I'm going to love this line because it says that my song shall still be, "Let me be nearer, my God, to thee."

One of my top-ten favorite hymns is "Draw Me Nearer" ("I Am Thine, O Lord"). Many of you know that one. I find myself singing it many mornings while I'm getting ready – out loud if no one else is in the house! It truly is my sincere prayer for every day – to edge a bit closer to my blessed Lord and to the cross where he died.

The next time you stand to sing in worship, whatever your musical style, realize that your songs to the crucified, risen Christ are still genuine – after all these years. May ALL our songs still continue to draw us nearer to the One who is now on heaven's throne at the top of those steps where angels beckon us to come. May our thoughts and attitudes truly still be brightened with his praise.

Try your best to stop thinking of this as a hymn about a mighty ship going down; rather, consider a mighty church rising up in praise, still moving nearer to one another and their Captain.

57 Guide Me, O Thou Great Jehovah

Tune: CWM RHONDDA
Text: William Williams (1717-1791)

"Bread of heaven, feed me till I want no more."

"I am the bread of life that has come down from heaven. The one who comes to me will never go hungry, and those who believe in me will never be thirsty." This "I Am" quote of Jesus from John 6:35 gives us the starting place for today's hymn line.

Is it possible for Christ to feed us to the point of wanting no more of his nourishment? Can we gorge ourselves on the truth of who Christ is until we say, "That's all I can take?" Somehow, I don't think so. Admittedly, I have never over-indulged at Christ's table; I have snacked, selectively dined, taken the 'pick and choose' approach; I have rarely feasted on the Bread of heaven or over-imbibed from the fruit of the true Vine.

I've over-done church before. I have gotten to the point that I've had all the committee meetings and the rehearsals I could bear. I've given myself in mission and outreach until I thought I had no more to give. I've been to the point I want nothing else to do with church folk.

But I have yet to binge on the person of Jesus… so full of who he is and what he wants to teach me that I cry "uncle"!

Come to the table. Feast on Jesus until you have to loosen your belt! Devour every facet of his nature and replicate that in your life. Then you can sing with great sincerity, "Bread of heaven, feed me till I want no more."

Isn't it about time we get fed up with Jesus?

58 The Church's One Foundation

Tune: AURELIA
Text: Samuel E. Stone (1839-1900)

*"Her charter of salvation:
one Lord, one faith, one birth."*

The Beatles sang, "One is the loneliest number…"; however, this hymn's second stanza negates that sentiment, reminding us that people from every nation are now one… world-wide, that the church blesses one holy name and partakes one holy food, and that we press forward in one united hope. The centerpiece statement about our one-ness is today's hymn line: we share one Lord, one faith, and one birth… actually one re-birth!

Most every organization has a charter – a document which sets out its basic purpose. The charter declares "why" this group is being formed; from its very beginning, these people are associating themselves toward this end… or these commitments. According to Samuel Stone's hymn which crosses all denominational lines, the charter of the church (made up of people who share in the salvation of Christ) is to share
• only one Lord – that is Christ himself
• one common faith – a reliance on that same Christ… an ultimate trust in him
• a one-time, born-again experience.

Probably no other single stanza speaks more directly to the unity of the church. In thirty-nine words, our commonality is underscored; every time we sing those thirty-nine words, the One Word is highlighted as we recommit ourselves to the basic charter of our salvation – a charter which unites and does not divide.

So, one is NOT the loneliest number. In fact, we are never alone when we cast our lot with other believers, other pilgrims on the journey. And we are never looking out for "number one" (ourselves), because that would not be in keeping with the example modeled for us by our One Lord. Instead, we are looking out for the real "Number One," in our worship, our fellowship, and our ministry.

Unlike some sports fans in the stands, the only foam finger we need is one that points to Christ, who is still our One Foundation.

59 When Christ Was Lifted from the Earth

Common Tune: ST. BOTOLPH
Text: Brian Wren (1936-   )

"He sees not labels but a face, a person and a name." [8]

One of the most insightful hymn writers of the 20th Century into this century is Brian Wren. As one who applies himself to the penning of an occasional hymn or anthem text, I marvel at Wren's ability to word his faith so bluntly and creatively.

In this hymn line, Wren speaks a loud and clear word of acceptance, saying that Christ overlooks the human-attached labels and sees instead the individual – the face, the person, the name. I believe that is exactly how Christ observes all people… and I am convinced that his example of acceptance should be imitated by those of us who say that we are followers of the King. [By the way, He concludes the hymn with an admonition to accept as Christ has accepted us.]

Probably no group on earth is more involved in the needless act of labeling than the Christian community… especially the more fundamental, narrow fringes. Why do we do that? What gives us the right to overlook the "judge not" passages? (Matthew 7:1, Luke 6:37, etc.) Even those of us who would never voice our label-attachments may mentally do so. Shame on us!

It's something we need to stop doing… and we need to speak out against those who do. Tagging is not Christlike behavior – accepting by grace is. If the perfect One can look beyond our faults, shouldn't we do that to our fellow strugglers?

I also like the way Wren says that Christ sees a face, a person, and a name. That tells me that if I get to know some of the people whom I might be inclined to brand – if I got to know their name, their circumstance, their plight – I might be less inclined.

This is a powerful, needed message for those of us who are serious about acting out our faith. Even though it is tucked away in the middle

→

of a hymn you may not know, it should leap off the page and into our hearts to change us if need be.

I've heard that we should always err on the side of grace. This hymn line echoes that adage.

---

60 All Hail the Power of Jesus' Name

Tunes: DIADEM, MILES LANE, CORONATION
Text for This Stanza by John Rippon (1751-1836)

"Let every kindred, every tribe on this terrestrial ball,
to him all majesty ascribe
and crown him Lord of all."

I know it was politically incorrect, but as a child we sang, "Red and yellow, black and white, they are precious in his sight." Even as a youngster, I learned from a simple song that we are all in this together, regardless of our race, our kinfolk, or our lineage. I've tried to maintain that attitude... and have extended those groupings and moved the stakes out further until the tent can contain us all.

This hymn line conjures up for me another one of those mental pictures. In this one, I see a multi-colored throng of all the world's people standing together in what in my mind at least looks like a huge city square; I would say it looks sort of like the plaza in front of St. Peter's Cathedral, but I know somebody would be offended that I had a Catholic vision! Anyway, all those people are singing at the top of their lungs, but their fortissimo-singing is very much under control. It's not yelling; the sound is very, very musical. They are all lifting up their praise to the One who sits on the throne.

For a brief moment during the singing of this great hymn, I am transported into that scene where I join the everlasting song... and I realize what a wonderful place it is... and will be. This is not something we have to wait for; we can stand shoulder to shoulder with our fellow believers from every background, race, gender, lifestyle, and denomination to honor the One who loves us all and equally accepts our ascription of praise. So let's.

61 We Are Gathered for Thy Blessing

Tune: TABERNACLE
Text: Paul Rader (1878-1938)

"Bring us low in prayer before thee."

This hymn was written by a Denver-born American preacher who became the first radio evangelist. In today's hymn line, Rader brings to our minds the New Testament parable about the Pharisee and the tax collector. I don't usually include a Scripture passage, but here I think we need to be reminded of the details:

> *A Pharisee and a tax collector went up to the Temple to pray. The Pharisee stood up and prayed all about himself: "God, I thank you that I am not like other people--robbers, evildoers, adulterers--or even like this tax collector. I fast twice a week and give a tenth of all I get."*
> *But the tax collector stood over to the side and would not even look up to heaven, but beat his chest and said, "God, have mercy on me, sinner that I am."*
> *I tell you that this tax collector, rather than the proud-talker, went home justified before God. For everyone who exalts himself will be humbled, and the one who humbles himself will be exalted. [Luke 18:10-14]*

This posture of humility… not even looking up when praying… was the more acceptable prayer – elegant in its attitude and simplicity.

"Prostrate" is a good worship word we use that helps us picture "bring us low in prayer before thee." It means falling flat on your face… sprawled out on the floor… getting as low as you can in the presence of God… avoiding any possibility of arrogance or entitlement.

When we were in Rome recently, we happened upon a church that was home to a small sect of believers whose worship was done prostrate on the floor before the altar. We were in the small basilica when one of their prescribed worship times began and were witnesses to their unusual ritual. As odd as it was for a pretty staid American Baptimethoterian, I was fascinated and moved by the way they so seriously lowered their bodies and lay face-down in the Presence for an extended period of time. →

These give us mental pictures, but the point to all this is not so much the physical positioning as the heart posture. With as little hubris as possible, we approach the throne in such an unassuming way that our cries for mercy might be heard, and we might go on our way "justified before God."

So, how low can you go?

62

It's So Wonderful

Tune: COBBS
Text and Music: Ralph H. Good Pasteur (1923-1996)

"I join in the singing for I can't decline." [9]

Some of us (mostly men) will recall the great fear that came along with us when we went to high school dances… okay, "sock hops" for some of us whose parents wouldn't let us associate with an event that involved the gyrations of social dancing. As long as we were just hopping about in our bobby socks, it seemed more acceptable! Back to that fear thing: The fear was not in ASKING someone to dance with us as much as it was in the possibility – even likelihood – that they would DECLINE.

Along life's pilgrimage, we have made the choice to decline many offers far beyond a three-and-a-half-minute dance. Most of us have turned down job offers, move-away opportunities – for some, even wedding proposals. Declining is usually a polite refusal, not an act of spiteful spurning.

As someone who loves to sing in church – especially the great hymns – I have always been taken aback by the cross-armed refusal of some (again, mostly men) to participate. Some do this because they've been told they don't sing well, some because it's not the 'manly' thing to do, some because they find the music portion of the service to be a waste of time… for others, it's just plain old obstinacy! Let those refuse to sing who never knew our God, but children of the heavenly King may – no, "must" - speak their joys abroad as they march upward to Zion.

I remember the first time I ever sang the spirited spiritual "It's So Wonderful": It was at Glorieta, New Mexico, in Holcomb Auditorium as William J. Reynolds introduced us to the new BAPTIST HYMNAL 1975. I recall the joy that permeated the room as a predominantly white congregation of three thousand worshipers was introduced to such a wonderful 20th Century African-American praise song. Few stood arm-folded! Most swayed, clapped the beat, smiled; not many lifted-hands were spotted because this WAS 1975 and we were Baptists after all!

Imagine (here I go again!) the Lord Christ walking up to you and asking you if you care to sing – if you would like to join in the verbalizing of your faith – to participate in praise of the one who invites you. Is there any way on earth you might say, "No thanks. I'd rather just stand here and listen"? I somehow doubt it.

We are made that offer every time we gather as a worshipping community. The next time Jesus approaches you across a crowded room and reaches out his hand and says, "Wanna dance… or sing?", don't you dare decline! Uncross those arms (even lift them if you are so inclined) and cut loose in vibrant praise. It will make you both feel better.

From "Dance at Bougival" – Pierre-Auguste Renoir

Break Thou the Bread of Life

Tune: BREAD OF LIFE
Text: Mary A. Lathbury (1841-1913)

"Beyond the sacred page I see thee, Lord."

Finding God beyond the written Word is part of the Christian maturing process.

There was a time in most of our lives when we looked only to scripture to find what God was saying to us or doing around us. When you're in Sunday School and Vacation Bible School, there is so much emphasis on the Bible itself that we zero in on that book when we are looking for God and his answers to our dilemmas. That's not a bad thing, but it IS a very limited approach.

I still have the Bible I first carried with me to church – partly to read, partly to be able to check "Bible Brought" on my offering envelope! It was black leather and had a zipper to protect the pages. It did not have those little tabs that helped you find the books of the Bible because my mother thought one should find those on their own; she was, after all, the associational director of the Sword Drill. (Ask a middle-aged Baptist if you don't know what that is!) The Book that contained God's message to his people was very important to me – still is.

Somewhere along my spiritual journey I realized that God spoke to me beyond the sacred pages... that I could find him very much alive in nature... that I could see him in the lives of people around me and hear him in their words of encouragement and teaching. As long as what those people were doing and saying was in keeping with the teachings of that little zippered black book, I could be enriched and edified by human interaction.

The communicating faithful led me to think outside the book... beyond the sacred page. They widened my horizons and helped me turn some important corners in my pilgrimage of faith.

Lots of people write lots of books and are on lots of television and radio shows, producing lots of video series, etc. Most of them are doing that for the right reasons, I'm sure – and I've learned many things from them. But it's the everyday genuine FOJ – follower of Jesus – whose life and comments continue to shape my walk.

When I sing this hymn line, I visualize myself looking over the top edge of a page, beyond the zipper's regular pattern to see God. In other words, I hear him in other words… and see him in other faces.

Thankfully, beyond Revelation 22:21, I see you, Lord.

64 Spirit of God, Descend upon My Heart

Tune: MORECAMBE
Text: George Croly (1780-1860)

**"Stoop to my weakness, mighty as thou art,
and make me love thee as I ought."**

George Croly was an Irish poet, novelist, historian and Anglican priest. In spite of all his writings, this is his only hymn commonly included in Christian hymnals. I can identify!

I love the imagery of an adult bending down to lift up a child; it seems to be a common theme throughout hymnody. This one, however, seems a little more "grown up" and comes across more as a desperate plea for rescue from one's weak estate, with full realization that the Spirit of God is strong enough to come to our aid. This might remind us of another hymn line: "I am weak, but thou art strong."

The next line could almost be troubling: "And make me love thee as I ought to love." We need not look at the word "make" as an activity performed against our will – like Flip Wilson's "The Devil made me do it!" Here, it seems to me that we who are salvaged from our feebleness are asking that our response might be to love the One who bends down to free us… to save us from what seems like an inexorable, helpless condition. Perhaps we should look at it more as an artist who makes his/her media into something else – remakes clay into a vessel, paint into a portrait, sounds into music… or words into poetry which eventually becomes a hymn for congregational singing.

Admitting weakness, crying out for recovery, allowing transformation to occur. This is a pretty good pattern for rededicating one's life.

65 Jesus, the Very Thought of Thee

Tune: ST. AGNES
Text: 12th Century Latin Hymn
Translated by Edward Caswall (1814-1878)

"No voice can sing, no heart can frame,
nor can the memory find
a sweeter sound than thy blest name."

What is it about the very speaking of the name of Jesus that warms us like it does? Or why is it when we hear someone using his name as a form of swearing that we are so chilled to the bone? Unless you're sitting at your desk at work surrounded by lots of other people, take a minute and speak that wonderful name of Jesus out loud a few times… naturally, not forced… as if you were talking to him face to face, starting or ending a sentence with that declaration.

Now wasn't that brilliant? Isn't it magnificent to magnify the precious name of Jesus? To quote Bill and Gloria Gaither, "There IS just something about that name." [10]

But even better is when those two syllables are intoned… sung! That is why congregational singing is one of the most electrifying experiences we Christians can enjoy together. Truly, when we sing, "Jesus, Jesus, Jesus: sweetest name I know! It fills my ev'ry longing and keeps me singing as I go," something in us is stirred because for those of us to whom singing is a priority, we have sung exactly what we believe!

As whole-heartedly as we may try to express (frame) our faith, words will never do. We can bring back to mind some of the greatest sounds we've encountered during our entire lives, but even then we cannot seem to find a sweeter sound than those two syllables.

Ponder these three lines, praying them one at a time:
- *In my best voice, I am not able to sing a sweeter sound than thy blest name, O Savior.*
- *My heart cannot frame (construct) a sweeter sound than thy blest name, O Savior.*

- *Nowhere in my memory can I find a sweeter sound than thy blest name, O Savior.*

This hymn-writer said it so well, so succinctly – so beautifully. That's why when we stumble across this kind of hymnody, we are drawn back to it over and over again. And I am here to remind you why!

---

66   I Am His, and He Is Mine

Tune: EVERLASTING LOVE
Text: George W. Robinson (1838-1877)

"Something lives in every hue
Christ-less eyes have never seen."

Listening to NPR the other day, they were discussing color, of all things. Part of their discussion was that most people don't pay much consideration to color until someone or something draws their attention to it. In other words, because most of us see in vivid colors, we just take them for granted, not noticing how the hues of our surroundings contribute to our enjoyment of all we see.

When the interviewee said that, I was driving out in the country; and suddenly, the greens got greener and the yellows got yellower. I noticed how bright blue the sky looked. Even the farm houses began to pop out at me.

I teach art appreciation classes at the college where I add junk… I mean where I'm an adjunct professor. I'm all the time telling my students to notice sounds, shapes, symmetry, and yes – color. I sometimes demonstrate that by displaying colorless paintings or photographs over against those that appear in living color! So I, of all people, should be more aware.

The line which precedes this hymn line says that because I am his, and he is mine, heaven above is softer blue, and earth around is sweeter green. The statement which follows is about how birds with gladder songs o'erflow, and flow'rs with deeper beauties shine. I think Robinson is trying to point out that our closer-related association with

→

Christ should make us more aware of the simplest, most beautiful things. We should have our 'feelers out' and be more sensitive to all good gifts… even the simplest, most basic which are missed by those whose Christ-less eyes have not ever noticed.

Our proximity to Christ opens us up to many blessings; on that, we probably all agree. But this hymn line calls our attention to some of the lesser-religious ones – yet very sacred!

Today, notice the sounds, the shapes, smells and colors with more intention. Not because it's an art class assignment, but because you are his and he is yours. I'm going to try to do that myself – O thou who pointeth all this out to thy students – since I know as now I know I am his and he is mine.

---

67   O Love That Will Not Let Me Go

Tune: ST. MARGARET
Text: George Matheson (1842-1906)

***"And feel the promise is not vain
that morn shall tearless be."***

Several years ago, in front of a sanctuary filled with well-dressed wedding attendees, America's hymn-singer, recording artist Cynthia Clawson forgot the words to this hymn. She sang the first phrase and then began to hum and 'ooh' her way through her favorite hymn... and indeed, one of mine.

It was the wedding ceremony of Carlita Lowry and R. G. Huff. There we stood in the middle of the platform with Wayne Jenkins officiating, and Carla Lowry and Billy Coburn as our maid of honor/best man. A choir loft filled with singers who had just gloriously sung the Beethoven "Hallelujah" from THE MOUNT OF OLIVES under the direction of my seminary roommate David Lane all had their eyes fixed on us. And Cynthia kept ad libbing! Like the text of the hymn, we were transferred from weeping to laughter. Later she said, "I knew it had something to do with water, but I couldn't remember what!" It's a story for another book.

To put this hymn line into context:

> *O joy that seekest me through pain,*
> *I cannot close my heart to thee.*
> *I trace the rainbow through the rain*
> *And feel the promise is not vain*
> *That morn shall tearless be.*

The joy of the Lord is my strength, and it comes looking for me when I'm in pain or despair. When it finds me, it makes me an offer I cannot refuse - I open my heart to be renewed by the joy of my salvation. Realizing such complete renewal, I visualize the rainbow that arcs *apres pluie* - after rain - reminding me of the promise of God that a morning will come when there will be no tears... only this presence of joy.

"Tears may linger throughout the darkness, but our joy comes with the morning light." Psalm 30:5 (RgV)

I've never been able to sing that entire stanza without tearing up... usually choking up. These tears, however, are not the painful, dark-time saline drops; these are tears prompted by the joy that continues to come looking for me to remind me that none of God's promises are wasted on his people... on me!

On August 1, 1992, at University Baptist Church in Denver (no longer in existence, by the way), Carlita and I made promises to one another, to God, and to the great cloud of witnesses who shared our wedding day. Those promises to love, to be faithful, to endure - those promises continue to bring joy to our lives; and this long hymn line applies to our marriage, and I could easily sing it to her as well as to Christ: I cannot close my heart to thee.

Watch for the rainbows. Let the prismic phenomena remind you that there is a love that will not give up on you. Rest your weary soul in that truth.

Joy is always right on your heels. Slow down and let it catch up with you.

68   God Moves in a Mysterious Way

Tune: ST. ANNE
Text: William Cowper (1731-1800)

*"God is his own interpreter,
and he will make it plain."*

This is definitely one of those 'tucked away' hymn lines; it is usually the final line of this hymn as printed in most hymnals. I like it when the last line of a hymn is the one the grabs me - the 'hook,' so to speak - because I can really stop and think.

One of the things I miss most in the evolution of contemporary worship is the trend to avoid silence. Every moment seems to need filler of some kind. However, when we have sung a text like this one, we might ought to turn off the sound system for a minute or two and chain the ministers to their chairs so the rest of us can reflect on what we just sang: "God is his own interpreter, and he will make it plain." Some churches who still follow an order of worship include the times listed as "Silence is kept." This should be one of those times.

Don't you love it when you're watching someone sign - interpret for the deaf - during a concert, and as you watch them, the songs are made more understandable... their interpretation makes the message more plain?

"Who has known the mind of the Lord? Who his counselor ever became?" (Romans 11:34) This scripture passage comes to mind as I think on this hymn line. Really: Who knows what God is thinking? Who would ever try to give him advice? Who would have ever attempted to explain to Einstein what $E=mc2$ means? Who would have advised Michelangelo to use a little more green on the ceiling of the Sistine Chapel? Who would have suggested an alternate ending to "Romeo and Juliet"?

We wouldn't do that because we trust that these geniuses knew what they were doing. So why would we question the ways of God -THE Genius of all geniuses, King of all kings, Lord of all lords.

Certainly, we don't understand all that God does - universally or in our own lives. But we can be certain that nobody tells him what to do, and none of us should try to totally figure him out. It is the continuing mystery of God that intrigues us; it may well be what sets him apart as the God of all gods.

Babbie Mason wrote a song that says simply, "When you can't trace his hand, trust his heart." [11] [Silence is kept.]

Today and the rest of our days, let's stay out of God's business when it comes to how he rules his kingdom; let's let him interpret himself. We may not 'get it' now, but eventually it will come to light - the truth be told. At the same time, let's be about our Father's business! Meanwhile, to quote another old gospel song, "We will understand it better by and by."

O God, maintain your mystery. Amen.

---

69   I Am Thine, O Lord

Tune: I AM THINE
Text: Fanny J. Crosby (1820-1915)

"O the pure delight of a single hour that before thy throne I spend."

O the pure delight of a single hour
that before thy throne I spend
When I kneel in prayer, and with thee, my God,
I commune as friend with friend.

There is not a whole lot I can add to that. This hymn line speaks for itself.

Our understanding of prayer as a communication between friends makes a lot of difference in how we approach the throne. Prayer is not a duty, it is a privilege – one that should be cherished and anticipated, much like we look forward to catching up with our dearest friends.

→

There are no off-limits subjects, we talk about everything and anything, we are at ease, there is no sense of tension.

My seminary roommate and I have talked by phone every Monday for years. It is a loosely scheduled weekly catching-up time. These sometimes-brief conversations continue to be a blessing. I'm trying to reshape my prayer life to be more like my visits with David: just talking to God and asking him for nothing. Too much of my prayer time is centered around what I want God to do for me. I'm trying to alter that… or altar that!

Spending an hour in prayer is probably a stretch for most of us, but whatever time we carve out to dedicate to dialogue with this great Friend should be delightful. Some days I may visit with God an hour… five minutes at time! But those occasional intense, lengthy audiences are the richest because they yield superior results. O the pure delight…

---

70   My Lord, I Did Not Choose You

Various Tunes
Text: Josiah Conder (1789-1850)

*"Unless your grace had called me
and taught my opening mind,
the world would have enthralled me."*

This may be a hymn text you have never sung. I admit that I have not sung it too frequently over the years, but when I have, THIS is the hymn line that catches my attention.

First, it reminds me that the amazing grace of Christ called me into and taught me about the kingdom. The luring power of God's grace may have been like the siren's song – only this was a positive melody that pulled me not into dangerous waters or a swirling eddy, but rather into the safest of all waters.

I sincerely hope that I have an ever-more-open mind… that my perspective on all things spiritual and corporeal – even cultural – is constantly expanding. I attribute that ever-widening of my horizons to my deeper understanding of grace during my pilgrimage of faith.

When I sing this hymn line, I picture that opening of Monty Python's Flying Circus where the top of the man's head is flipped open and stuff goes pouring in. I realize we have to filter our thinking and guard our mind, but it doesn't have to be slammed shut, locked tight against all other ways of thinking, doing, and living.

Were it not for grace, the world would have lured me with its siren song, and mine might have been an entirely different path than it has turned out to be. I might well have been dashed upon the rocks, spinning in an eddy like I found myself one summer afternoon when thrown from a raft into "the widow maker" on the Arkansas River in Colorado.

Do you remember the story of Pinocchio? At least you might recall the 1940 Disney film. Most of us think of the growing-nosed-liar of a wooden marionette, but the scenes that flash through my mind while singing today's hymn line is when Pinocchio decides he is grown up enough to head out on his own, out from under his creator Geppetto's constant care. He finds himself much like the Prodigal Son; instead of a pig-pen, Pinocchio and his friends go to Pleasure Island where they gamble, smoke and get drunk – obviously not good church kids! A curse actually turns them into jackasses!

This fairy tale has a lot of biblical implications, including characters being swallowed and coughed-up by a whale. It also has the re-uniting of the father-figure with his wayward whittling project of a boy. In the end, Pinocchio dies and is brought back to life, being reborn as a human after all – no longer lumbering his way through life.

But I digress. The world outside Geppetto's workshop and the sin he discovered on Pleasure Island – these enthralled him. With wide-eyed wonder, he wanted to try it all.

We're all familiar with the phrase: "There but by the grace of God go I" (attributed to 16th Century preacher/martyr John Bradford). That pretty much sums up this hymn line, doesn't it?

Creator of who I am: Keep calling me by your grace to be open-minded, but don't let me be so enthralled by my bedazzled surroundings to lose sight of the One who made me and who severed the strings so I could discover who I would be and who I have become. Amen.

I Saw the Cross of Jesus

Tune: WHITFIELD
Text: Frederick Whitfield (1829-1904)

*"In every trying hour, my sure and certain refuge,
my never-failing tower."*

I'm the artistic director for Waxahachie's Old-Fashioned Singing Project, a local non-profit. One of the American brush-arbor gospel songs we sing is "Where Could I Go but to the Lord?" When we sing today's hymn line in worship, I revert to my growing-up roots and am reminded of that old gospel song - because the message is basically the same.

In every trying hour, the cross of Christ seems to rise from the situation and become a sure and certain refuge, my never-failing tower. It's the place I turn to. After all, where else could I go? Why would I go anywhere else? If that refuge - that secure place - that safe room - is available to me, why should I keep trying to hide out in a less-protected place?

In today's society, I'm offered many escape routes when life is going haywire on me - or when I am sinking deep in sin. Any of those which are not in the shadow of the cross are probably not best for me.

Proverbs 18:12 - *"The name of the Lord is a strong tower; the righteous run into it and find safety."* It is that place where I am safe and secure from all alarms.

Most of us can count on one hand - maybe on one finger - everything in our lives that are sure, certain and never-failing. I'll give you a moment to calculate that. When you've completed that assignment, I hope that the cross and One whose life was taken and freely given there are on your list - at the top - maybe the only ones on your list!

A television-commercial-promoted product may claim to be 'all that,' but only that dear dying Lamb can truly live up to that kind of promise. He is my sure and certain, unassailable shelter in the time of storm - a tower to which I can run for safety, slam the door behind me and feel perfectly defended from whatever is chasing me. You've heard of being "out of harm's way"? This is it. Look no further.

Where could I go but to the Lord? Why should I? Why would I?

Why Do I Sing about Jesus?

Tune: KETCHUM
Text and Music: Albert A Ketchum (1894-1984?)

"Grace, love and pity he shows."

Grace and love are pretty familiar church terms because they are tossed about freely in our sermons, Bible studies, hymns and songs. If asked what two attributes of God are favorites, most would probably respond with these two. I, for one, consider the grace (or mercy) of God to be at the top of my list. [See entry 18 for the list of attributes of God.]

This hymn line, however, employs a less-often uttered term among us believer-types. Perhaps because none of us wishes to be pitied by another, we avoid the word. "She's just pitiful" or "It's a pitiful mess he's gotten himself into" are phrases we'd rather not have spoken about us.

But "pity" is great descriptor of the kind of grace and love expressed in the example of Christ. Pity is simply a substitute term for compassion… especially compassion that is felt because another is suffering some kind of loss or misfortune. One of the definitions I came across was a "fellow feeling" – a shared understanding of what another is going through.

It is not at all positional: a looking down upon. It is not objective: viewed from a distance as we wag our heads and say, "Oh, you pitiful person." Instead, it is identifying with another, putting ourselves on the same level… standing on even ground with all human strugglers.

In the life, ministry and teachings of Jesus, we find these three things on display… always. Because he is our example, we should set out to exhibit these three… always!

Stop using "pity" in a negative context; move that term over to your positive column. Approach the one who stands before you as a fellow-feeler. Even if you haven't faced the same difficulty or dilemma, you can identify with having been a deflated wanderer who – for some period of time – lived as one without hope.

"Grace, love and pity he shows." It is show-time for the rest of us!

He Keeps Me Singing

Tune: SWEETEST NAME
Text and Music: Luther Bridgers (1884-1948)

"Always looking on his smiling face, that is why I shout and sing."

Have you ever noticed how much difference a smiling face makes? We all know it is always better to smile than to scowl, but sometimes we Christians forget!

We were at the local Chili's recently. Our buzzer went off to let us know our table was ready, and as we vacated the little bench we had occupied for several minutes, a gentleman – no, there was nothing gentle about this man – almost knocked us down taking our obviously much-coveted spot by the bar. I glanced in his direction and held back from saying what I wanted to say lest a Texas bar fight break out, and he had the ultimate unhappy, mad-at-the-world look on his face. I admit, I didn't give him a smile, but just kept following the hostess to our table.

I wondered to myself if that guy had probably been in church a few hours earlier, singing in the choir, taking up the offering, or (God forbid) standing in the pulpit!

All of that to say that we who represent Christ in the world should have a visage that matches his... that compassionate, pleasant look that we all seem to share with newborns and small children. It is often a look that we don't share as often with our peers.

While feasting on the riches of his grace and resting beneath his sheltering wings, I keep my attention on his smiling face which gives me good reason to shout and sing. So says the song.

If you have seen the smiling face of Jesus, pass it along to someone else. Pay it forward. Make sure you don't grab it and hold it for yourself, your children/spouse, or the people who accompany you to weekly worship. You may even have to smile at some guy who topples you in the waiting area of a local restaurant!

See Jesus' smile? Share it regularly.

There's a Glad New Song

Tune: REDEEMING LOVE
Text and Music: Albert C. Fisher (1886-1946)

"When at last I stand with the heavenly choir…
I shall never tire." [12]

For the first time in over forty years, I recently sang in a church choir! I experienced the music ministry from the other side of the rail! I consider myself fortunate indeed to have attended an evangelical church that still has a choir; the truth is that church has had several people join because they want to attend a service in which the music is choir-driven.

It's a very good choir: they sing well, read music better than most volunteer groups, and they are engaged in their leadership of worship. Another way in which I am fortunate is that the minister of music is a great person, wonderful minister and a good friend.

But one of these days, I plan to stand with a massive number of singers who gather near the throne of God to offer up continual praise of the One who sits there! I have the feeling the music never ends – that it'll be like an incessant medley, won't it? When we finish one great hymn or anthem, we'll modulate into the next. For us musicians, THAT would be heavenly!

Although it sounds like an old gospel song, the third stanza of this fairly new hymn (first published in 1956, ten years after the death of its writer) speaks to me with today's hymn line and following:

When at last I stand with the heav'nly choir
in the light of the throne above,
On the golden strand I shall never tire
of the song of redeeming love!
Of his love I shall ever sing
Till above I behold the King.
Through eternity my glad song shall be
of the Savior's redeeming love.

You may be like I've been sometimes: flying into the choir room after Sunday School and throwing on a robe, making certain you have the

→

correct stole turned to the right side, grabbing a folder and racing to a chair, trying your best to be situated before the pre-service rehearsal begins. I have often audibly said "Whew" as my backside hit the chair. But once the singing began, I was always renewed.

I hope I shall never tire of singing the praises of God… in this life or the next.

---

75   Praise to the Lord, the Almighty

Tune: LOBE DEN HERREN
Text: Joachim Neander (1650-1680)
Translated by Catherine Winkworth (1827-1878)

"Ponder anew what the Almighty can do."

For most of us, our daily lives do not allow us much time to ponder. In fact, pondering may be becoming a lost art.

In the context of this hymn line, pondering requires our being still and knowing that God is God... and that he can achieve anything as the Almighty, all-powerful, omni-able Lord of the universe. Reflecting on that fact allows us to believe that God can make a difference in the way things happen in the world, our community, our congregation.

For me, every time we pass over this phrase in a service of worship, I am encouraged to ponder not only what the Almighty can do all around me (bringing peace to the world, making it possible for hungry people to be fed, to make equality a reality, to work through the thought-processes of world leaders and church leaders, etc.), but also to consider what he can do in ME if I will allow him to.

I honestly think that most of us – even we who consider ourselves deeply religious people – have never grasped "what the Almighty can do." If we understood that and ran with it, our lives would be changed in ways we can't even imagine... and possibly in ways we couldn't accept!

This simple seven-word phrase calls us to renew our sense of wonder at what can be accomplished by the Almighty One. There was a time early on in our Christian pilgrimage when we truly believed God could do anything; we marveled at the possibilities as we sat in a circle in the "beginner's class" in Sunday School. But somewhere, along with everything else about our lives, we became jaded... somewhat less awe-struck by the mightiness of God. Some of us may have begun to think of him as the Somewhat-mighty God.

So let's you and I get away from the hub-bub for a few minutes – or even hours – and ponder the greatness of God, and let's do it: "Ponder (think seriously about) anew (afresh, like you once did) what the Almighty (the One who has all the power) can do (achieve, accomplish - around me and in me)."

It really could make a difference.

End Notes

1 – "When in Our Music God Is Glorified" - Text by Fred Pratt Green
   © 1972 Hope Publishing Company, Carol Stream, IL 60188.
2 – "Stir Your Church, O God, Our Father" - Text by Milburn Price
   © 1970 Broadman Press – 127 Ninth Ave. N., Nashville, TN
   37234.
3 – "My Singing Is a Prayer" - Text by Novella D. Preston Jordan © 1964
   Broadman Press, 127 Ninth Ave. N., Nashville, TN 37234.
4- "God, Whose Purpose Is to Kindle" – Text by Elton Trueblood, from
   The Incendiary Fellowship ©1967 by Elton Trueblood.
   Permissions held by Harper and Row Publishers.
5 – "Serve the Lord with Gladness" – Text by B.B. McKinney © 1959
   Broadman Press – 127 Ninth Ave. N., Nashville, TN 37234.
6 – "Wherever He Leads, I'll Go" – Text by B.B. McKinney © 1936,
   1964, Broadman Press – 127 Ninth Ave. N., Nashville, TN 37234.
7 – "Eternal God, May We Be Free" – Text by Michael Dell © 1986
   Broadman Press -- 127 Ninth Ave. N., Nashville, TN 37234.
8 – "When Christ Was Lifted from the Earth" – Text by Brian Wren
   © 1980, Hope Publishing Company, Carol Stream, IL 60188.
9 – "It's So Wonderful" – Text by Ralph H. Good Pasteur © 1955, 1975,
   First Church of Deliverance, Chicago.
10 – "There's Something about That Name" – Text by Bill and Gloria
   Gaither © 1970, William J. Gaither.
11 – "Trust His Heart" – Text by Eddie Carswell and Babbie Mason
   © 1989 Dayspring Music/ Word.
12 – "There's a Glad New Song" – Text by Albert C. Fisher © 1956, 1984,
   Broadman Press, 127 Ninth Ave. N., Nashville, TN 37234.

Hymn Title Index

Hymn Line Index

R. G. Huff is semi-retired from 40-plus years of music ministry in local churches in Texas, Colorado, and Missouri, most recently serving University Baptist Church in Chapel Hill, NC.

A native of Pigeon Forge, Tennessee, he graduated from Carson Newman University with a major in biblical studies and minors in music and art; he holds a Masters of Church Music from Southwestern Seminary in Fort Worth, Texas.

R. G. is a published hymn-writer, lyricist and composer and has written extensively for professional magazines. He is an adjunct professor in the College of Fine Arts at Dallas Baptist University. He is also the creative director of Waxahachie's Old-Fashioned Singing Project and maintains worshipRx.com (a resource site for planning traditional worship) and continues to post regularly to his hymnlines.blogspot.com.

He and Carlita live in her hometown of Waxahachie, Texas – about 30 minutes south of Dallas. They have two adult sons/daughters-in-law [Clint/Sherry, Dustin/Laura] and three grandsons [Kyle, Carson and Jude], all who live nearby.

He loves traveling, reading, visiting museums, attending movies and live theater… and riding roller coasters.

R. G. has a real passion for congregational singing and enjoys sharing that passion with church groups and choirs in workshops and retreat settings as well as in worship.

HYMN LINES
Card Sets Available

12 Full-Color Cards in Each Set
[Each Card is 4" x 6" – Actual Size Below]

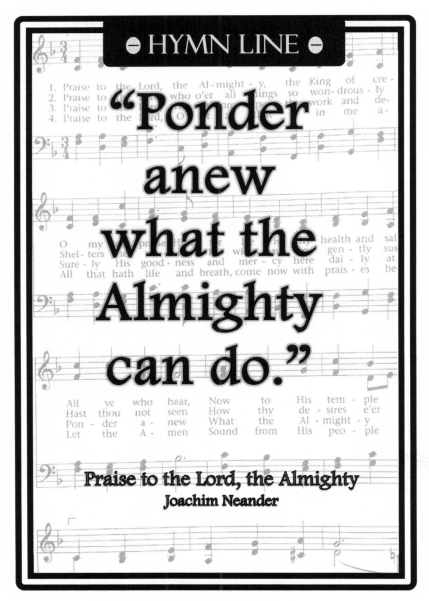

More details at WorshipRx.com

Order at WorshipRx.com

Set One	Set Two
Bread of heaven, feed me…	*Early let us seek thy favor…*
But while mortals rise & perish…	*Grace, love and pity he shows*
Do not be discouraged…	*He drew me closer to his side…*
Even when my heart is breaking…	*I cannot bear my burdens alone.*
Gushing from the rock…	*I sing for I cannot be silent.*
In heavenly love abiding…	*Mercy there was great…*
In my hand no price I bring…	*My sin, not in part…*
Ponder anew…	*O may my love to thee pure…*
Still… nearer, My God, to thee.	*Only thou art holy…*
The night becomes as day…	*Strength for today…*
Tune my heart to sing thy grace.	*Trusting in my Father's wise…*
When Jesus shows his smiling…	*We will rest where the steps…*

Put them on the piano, on the fridge, among the dishes, on your desk, by the sink… wherever you need to be reminded to sing!

Making My Son

Holy God of Wonder

Lad and Almighty

Mountains by dawn

Made in the USA
Monee, IL
09 August 2021